Difference
Difference
Difference
Difference
Makers

Difference
Makers

How to Live a Life of Impact & Purpose

GREGG MATTE

B&H
PUBLISHING
NASHVILLE, TENNESSEE

978-1-5359-5116-6

Published by B&H Publishing Group
Nashville, Tennessee

Dewey Decimal Classification: 128
Subject Heading: PROBLEM SOLVING \ LIFE \
DECISION MAKING

Unless otherwise noted, all Scripture quotations
are taken from the Christian Standard Bible®,
copyright © 2017 by Holman Bible Publishers. Used by
permission. Christian Standard Bible® and CSB® are
federally registered trademarks of Holman Bible Publishers.

Also used English Standard Version (ESV).
Text Edition: 2016. Copyright © 2001 by Crossway Bibles,
a publishing ministry of Good News Publishers.

Cover design by FaceOut Studio, Derek Thornton.

1 2 3 4 5 6 7 • 23 22 21 20 19

Dedication

I would like to dedicate this book to two Bry(i)ans who have been longtime difference makers in my life. Your listening ears when you have plenty on your own plate is a blessing.

First, Bryan Evans, my first cousin and just a few months apart in age and friends since the crib, you are more like a brother. Our weekly phone calls while one of us is driving down I-10, either filled with humor or leadership woes or wisdom, are so appreciated. Your insight and joy are a blessing to me! You are a great man.

Second, Brian Fisher, my fellow pastor and friend. You are a great encourager and source of insight and biblical perspective. Every pastor needs a buddy to call during sermon prep and ask, "Am I seeing this passage correctly?" Whether we are talking theology, church, family, or Jeeps. . . . I'm always inspired!

I'm grateful to both of you Bri(y)ans for the difference you are making in my life and my family's.

Lastly, it would be helpful if you guys could decide on how to correctly spell Bryan or is it . . . Brian?

Acknowledgments

Writing a book is a team effort. I'm so grateful for the LifeWay team around me, particularly my editor Taylor Combs for his hard work. Also, without the amazing inspiration of the people and staff of Houston's First Baptist Church this book would not be possible. Truly a church of difference makers! I'm thankful for my research team and our First Worship song-writing team who have partnered with LifeWay to create difference maker songs as a worshipful companion piece to the book. (Grab it at lifeway.com.)

Lastly, my wife, Kelly, and kids, Greyson and Valerie—affectionately called Team Matte—you are a source of fun and joy. You are my greatest earthly blessing. Truly difference makers in my life.

Contents

INTRODUCTION

Harvey

When the rain falls, the church rises. And on Sunday, August 27, 2017, it began to fall.

Hurricane Harvey began as a tropical wave in the Caribbean and grew into a tropical storm. By August 24, my birthday, it had become a hurricane. Not the gift I was looking for. On August 27 and 28, the city of Houston, where I live and pastor, received record rainfall of almost fifty inches![1] Entire counties in Texas were evacuated, airports were shut down for days, more than a hundred lives were lost, thousands upon thousands of homes, churches, offices, and schools were damaged, and some were completely destroyed. In our church alone there were more than seven hundred members and twenty-three staff members with homes flooded.

After we cancelled church on Sunday, I knew this one was going to be different. I got a late-night text message—church members from our Sienna campus were being evacuated from their neighborhood and needed a place to stay. I said, "If you can make it to my house, come on." In the wee hours of the morn they pulled in with their three kids, asleep in car seats, and all the stuff they could fit into their car.

Since our house was full, I arranged for our friends to stay with neighbors and church members on our street and around the corner. With tears in my eyes, standing in the driveway watching my neighbors retreat to their safe, dry homes with new guests they'd never met before, I knew something was different. But I could see the seeds of the church in action. This was going to be a big one. I knew I was going to have to do something. I knew our church was going to have to do something. And I began asking, "Lord, what's going to happen? What do we need to do?"

Can We Make a Difference?

It didn't take long to realize the city and surrounding towns were devastated. Thankfully, all of our church's campuses were dry and intact. Many of our members—myself included—were in homes largely unaffected by the storms. A great blessing, but clearly, it was a massive responsibility. I knew we had to do something, but the question was: *What can we do?* And even more so, in the face of seemingly incalculable damage and suffering, we were left asking: *Can we really make a difference?*

I've never seen anything quite like the weeks and months that followed. By the following Sunday, more than seventy-two thousand people had been rescued in Houston. Other churches who were unable to get into their buildings were worshiping with us, as we opened our doors to our neighbors. My sermon for the day was from two short verses:

> Blessed be the God and Father of our Lord Jesus Christ, the Father of mercies and the God of all comfort. He comforts us in all our affliction, so that we may be able to comfort those who are in any kind of affliction, through the comfort we ourselves receive from God. (2 Cor. 1:3–4)

Here's what I wanted our church to understand: we are blessed to be a blessing. We are comforted to be a comfort. In the good news of Jesus Christ, we had received the greatest comfort of all—the hope of salvation and the promise of eternal life with God. We knew that, through Christ, our sins had been forgiven. We knew that God had accepted us in Christ. In the midst of a world full of affliction, this is the greatest comfort, and by God's grace, we could take great joy in this comfort.

But we're not to be cul-de-sacs of God's comfort; we're to be conduits. The comfort of the gospel was never meant to get stuck in the church—it's meant to go *to* the church and then *to* the world *through* the church. Comforted to be a comfort. Blessed to be a blessing.

When I considered these verses penned by the apostle Paul, I knew the answer to my question: *Yes, we can make a difference.* And by God's grace, that's exactly what we did.

Becoming Difference Makers

This isn't to boast about our church or about myself. In fact, we were a very tiny piece of the puzzle of relief that came to Houston in the aftermath of Harvey. But we mudded out over a thousand homes, raised over two million dollars in relief funds, received donations that turned thousands of square feet of our church at all campuses into a distribution center, and we hosted countless people from near and far coming to serve, to help, to pray, to bring good news, to bring a cup of cold water, to bring relief. And that's exactly what it takes. When the rain falls, the church rises.

That's what it means to be a difference maker. Not that you can, by yourself, change the world, or that you can fix all the world's problems, but that Christians, one at a time, because of the gospel, join together to do *something*. We can each make a little difference *somewhere*. And all those little differences combined make a big difference. It did in Houston, and it's doing so all over the world.

This is my invitation to you: to become a difference maker. This is the hope of this book. I hope, as you read the following chapters and see stories from the Bible of all kinds of difference makers, that you'll realize that you've been called to do the same, and that you'll live into this calling.

Throughout this book, you'll find a common refrain. I call it The Difference Maker Declaration. We said this every Sunday for the year before Harvey hit and then we lived it more than ever. It's simultaneously a prayer and a commitment. I'm inviting you now to say this prayer, to make this commitment, and as you journey through this book and through your life, to return to these words, knowing this is the calling God has on your life:

> *I was made for more than watching. I have a history-changing, difference-making, life-giving, Spirit-empowered legacy to leave. Jesus, I ask you to work deeply in me and clearly through me as I pray, give, and go in your love. I am a difference maker. In Jesus' name. Amen.*

CHAPTER 1

Healthy Hearts

The leading cause of death in the United States is heart disease. In 2015, 633,842 American lives ended as a result of heart disease, almost a quarter of total deaths that year.[1] Dr. Steven Houser, president of the American Heart Association, believes "the future of cardiovascular research is to stop the disease before it starts."[2] Perhaps this goal explains the increasingly common labeling of various foods as "heart healthy." Salmon, almonds, blueberries, coffee, dark chocolate—all of these are now applauded as heart-healthy foods and recommended to include as part of your diet.

But is it too late to fix our massive problems with heart health as a country?

I'm eating healthier than I ever have, and let me tell you, it takes some discipline; I seem to like the taste of unhealthy foods! Some of this healthy stuff just doesn't do the trick for me. It seems nowadays like every meal in our house contains two ingredients: kale and cauliflower. What's the pizza crust made of, honey? Cauliflower. What are these pancakes made of? Cauliflower. What's in this sauce? Cauliflower. I finally decided to stop asking—I may enjoy the food more if I just don't know!

A Heart Problem

As serious as these heart-health issues are in our society, you and I come into the world with a heart problem that cannot be prevented. Ever since the first human beings, Adam and Eve, sinned, we have all come into this world with hard hearts. Instead of loving God and loving our neighbors, we love ourselves most of all. Instead of worshiping God and honoring him as Lord, we try to kick him off the throne and take it for ourselves. And because of this heart problem, we come into this world as God's enemies. It's not his fault—we're the ones who sin. And we make ourselves his enemies because of our sin.

What does this have to do with being a difference maker? You see, before you and I can be difference makers, a difference must be made in us. We need our unhealthy hearts to be replaced with healthy hearts.

Isaiah

The Old Testament book of Isaiah was written by the prophet Isaiah between the years 740 and 700 BC. Isaiah's ministry lasted through four kings: Uzziah, Jotham, Ahaz, and Hezekiah. The book has one major theme: _trust God_. In the Old Testament, Isaiah is a difference maker in the highest degree.

Isaiah was writing to people with hard hearts. They had a heart problem. They trusted in anything and everything before they trusted in God. They trusted in their own kings and their military. Then when that failed, they tried to make alliances with other nations so they could trust in those kings and militaries. They trusted in their external religion to keep God off their backs. But all the while, Isaiah is speaking to their hearts, trying to help them understand that their greatest need is to trust God.

The book of Isaiah shows us this right from the outset:

> Listen, heavens, and pay attention, earth, for the LORD has spoken: "I have raised children and brought them up, but they have rebelled against me. The ox knows its owner, and the donkey its master's feeding trough, but Israel does not know; my people do not understand. Oh sinful nation, people weighed down with iniquity, brood

of evildoers, depraved children! They have abandoned the LORD; they have despised the Holy One of Israel; they have turned their backs on him. (Isa. 1:2–4)

What's God saying to his people through Isaiah here? He's reminding them of his kindness and faithfulness to them. He gave them everything. He freed them from slavery in Egypt. He made them a nation. He brought them into the Promised Land, a land flowing with milk and honey. He gave them prosperity. But what did they do? They rebelled against God. They chose not to know him or honor him as their Father. They disobeyed his law and worshiped false gods. They abandoned him, despised him, and turned their backs on him.

God's announcing some bad news for Israel through Isaiah. Elsewhere in the Bible, he announces bad news for all of us. Psalm 14:2–3 says:

The LORD looks down from heaven on the human race to see if there is one who is wise, one who seeks God. All have turned away; all alike have become corrupt. There is no one who does good, not even one.

Those are universal statements. No one does good. No one seeks God. All have turned away.

So the Bible tells us that before we can make a difference in the world, a difference has to be made in us. But how? What can be done? If we keep reading the words of Isaiah, we'll find out.

Stop Doing Evil

The first thing Isaiah tells the Israelites is simple: stop sinning. Stop doing evil. Coming through loud and clear, Isaiah! Verse 16 says, "Wash yourselves. Cleanse yourselves. Remove your evil deeds from my sight. Stop doing evil."

When it comes down to it, sin is always the problem. Either love hinders sin in your life or sin hinders love. For the Israelites Isaiah was talking to—and for all of us when we come into this world—sin is always hindering love.

God is serious about sin. That is crystal clear in the book of Isaiah, as well as in the rest of the Bible. God is also serious about love. Many of us want God to be serious about love and not serious about sin. Others of us have this misconception about God where we think he's serious about sin and not serious about love. But God is serious about both. Why? Because he's holy.

Isaiah 6:3 says that God is "holy, holy, holy." This is a big deal. In our day, if we want to emphasize something in writing, we put it in italics or bold font or all caps. The authors of the Bible didn't have those luxuries, so when they wanted to emphasize something, they repeated it. For Isaiah to say God is "holy, holy, holy" is to say he's holy to the max.

Interestingly, this is the only characteristic of God in the Bible that is repeated three times like this. You never read "God is love, love, love," or "God is gracious, gracious, gracious." Certainly God is love (1 John 4:8), and he is gracious, merciful, kind, and compassionate. But he is also wrathful against sin, perfectly just, and promises to punish every sin ever committed. Here's the key to understanding this: all of God's characteristics flow from his perfect holiness.

For God to be perfectly holy means that he is totally set apart and completely perfect. Theologian Millard Erickson puts it this way:

> There are two basic aspects to God's holiness. The first is his uniqueness. He is totally set apart. . . . The other aspect of God's holiness is his absolute purity or goodness. This means that he is untouched and unstained by evil.[3]

In God's total otherness and his complete purity and perfection, he exercises all of his other characteristics: he acts with wrath and justice toward sin, he shows mercy and compassion, he loves. And he does all of these perfectly, in his complete holiness.

Therefore, God is serious about sin. Which means we need to be serious about sin. Which means we need to stop sinning. The Puritan pastor and author John Owen said, "Be killing sin or it will be killing you."[4] Sin always aims to kill us. It always wants to win. Unless we are seeking to kill sin, it will kill us.

Start Doing Good

There is a second change Isaiah tells his hearers they need to make: "Learn to do what is good. Pursue justice. Correct the oppressor. Defend the rights of the fatherless. Plead the widow's cause" (Isa. 1:17). Isaiah tells the Israelites not only to stop doing evil, but to start doing good.

We hear this and think immediately, *Oh, I've got to go to church more. I've got to work really hard to be religious. I've got to make a bunch of sacrifices for God so I can please him and get him off my back.* But the Lord knew that response was coming. In fact, it seems like the Israelites were already doing this. Look what God says to them:

> "What are all your sacrifices to me?"
> asks the LORD. "I have had enough of
> burnt offerings and rams and the fat of

well-fed cattle; I have no desire for the blood of bulls, lambs, or mail goats. . . . Stop bringing useless offerings. Your incense is detestable to me. New Moons and Sabbaths, and the calling of solemn assemblies—I cannot stand iniquity with a festival. . . . When you spread out your hands in prayer, I will refuse to look at you; even if you offer countless prayers, I will not listen. Your hands are covered with blood." (Isa. 1:11, 13, 15)

God was not interested in their religious actions or their "worship" experiences as long as they were still living in detestable sin. They were playing worship to get God off their backs, but they didn't really love him, and they certainly didn't love their neighbors. The essence of a difference-making heart is a growing love for God and others.

But we often do the same thing. Checking the religious boxes of a quiet time, church attendance, or prayer before dinner and bed. Our tithe is in the offering plate, but our heart is dreaming of the next Amazon Prime delivery. Do we actually love God and our neighbors, or do we just check boxes, doing what we "should"?

If we really love God, it will be evident in the way we love our neighbors, and this is what Isaiah's getting at here.

The actions of a loving, God-centered heart are to pursue justice, to correct the oppressor, to defend the rights of the orphans, and protect the widows. James 1:27 says, "Pure and undefiled religion before God the Father is this: to look after orphans and widows in their distress and to keep oneself unstained from the world." God, in Isaiah 1, called for his people to keep themselves unstained from the world (stop doing evil) and to look after orphans and widows (start doing good). He's calling for us to do the same.

Rest in the Finished Work of Christ

You might be feeling exhausted right now. You might not know where to start. You might be thinking to yourself: *I thought a relationship with God was about grace, but now I've got to do all this stuff?*

This is the beautiful part about Isaiah. Keep reading:

> "Come, let us settle this," says the LORD.
> "Though your sins are scarlet, they will be
> white as snow; though they are crimson
> red, they will be like wool." (Isa. 1:18)

This is the good news. This is a prediction of the cross. Seven hundred years before Jesus walked the face of the earth, God promised his people that he would remove their sins from them, and they would become pure.

How does this happen? Only by an exchange. Jesus came to trade places with us. He came and lived the life we failed to live and died the death we deserved to die so that we could be in a right relationship with God. Here's the sixty-four-dollar life-changing phrase from seminary: *substitutionary atonement.* Jesus stepped into our place to pay the ultimate price for our sin. He made the difference between eternal life and death by going to the cross for us. Wow!

You see, we can't stop doing evil and start doing good on our own. Something has to happen to us first. Our heart problem has to be fixed. Just a few books of the Bible later, God promises to do just that: "I will give you a new heart and put a new spirit within you; I will remove your heart of stone and give you a heart of flesh" (Ezek. 36:26). We need healthy physical hearts, so eat dark chocolate and blueberries and watch your cholesterol. But oh, how much more do we need healthy hearts spiritually! How much more do we need God to replace our hearts of stone and give us hearts of flesh.

John Owen, the seventeenth-century pastor quoted earlier, understood that to have the power to kill sin required one to have a relationship with Jesus. "Be sure to get an interest in Christ;" he said, "if you intend to mortify sin without it, it will never be done."[5] What did he mean by "interest"? He didn't mean interest like you might be interested in a good book or a show on Netflix. He meant interest in the economic sense, like an investment. When you're earning interest on something, it means you are connected to it in such a way that it is profiting you. When you get an interest in Christ, you are bound up with him, united to him by faith, and he grants you the power, through his Holy Spirit, to walk away from sin. An athlete in two-a-days is not growing stronger and flabbier at the same time. Closer to God is further from sin.

And he also enables you to do good. When God gives us a new heart, he gives us new affections. New desires. There was another Puritan named Thomas Chalmers who preached a sermon called "The Expulsive Power of a New Affection." Chalmers explains that when we are given healthy hearts, we have new affections—new loves and desires. Our old affections were self-centered and sinful; our new affections are centered in God and his glory. Now, we no longer want to keep sinning; we want to start doing good. We want to please God and bring glory to his name. Our new affections expel—kick out—our old affections. Psalm 37:4 says, "Delight yourself in the LORD, and he will give you the desires of your heart" (ESV), because now your desires are lining up with his.

This only happens because of the cross. Isaiah talked about exchanging our scarlet sins for white righteousness. The apostle Paul, in 2 Corinthians, said it this way: "He made the one who did not know sin to be sin for us, so that in him we might become the righteousness of God" (5:21). This is the gospel summarized in one sentence. The good news is what you might call a "double exchange." We exchange our sin for Christ's perfect righteousness, and he exchanges his righteousness for our sin. On the cross, he took on himself the punishment for our sin, and he gave us his righteousness, so that we can no longer be enemies of God, but sons and daughters of God. This is the difference that has to be made in us before we can be difference makers in the world.

But first, you have to trust God. Remember before when I said the whole message of Isaiah was about trusting God? That's really, in a sense, the message of the whole Bible. It's the message of the gospel. If you've trusted God, then you have a new heart. The gospel difference has already been made in you and you're ready to become a difference maker in the world. But if you haven't yet trusted God, you're still in your sin. You're still under his holy judgment. You're still his enemy.

The good news is that you don't have to stay that way. Jesus has made a way for you to become a son or a daughter of God. John 1:12 says, "But to all who did receive him, he gave them the right to be children of God, to those who believe in his name." Do you believe in Jesus? Do you believe that his death and resurrection were for you? To forgive your sins? To make you right with God? Receive this good news. Accept it. Let Jesus make a difference in your life. If you rest in his finished work, you'll be given a healthy heart, and you'll be ready to become a difference maker.

CHAPTER 2

What Does the World Need?

What does the world need more than anything else? It's a compelling question, and depending on one's culture, religion, and background, the answer may vary. Jason Clay, senior vice president for World Wildlife, argued in an essay for the *New York Times* that what the world needs most is education. "We must be on a relentless journey toward self-betterment," he argues. "We must ask questions of ourselves and the people and institutions around us, so as to increase our knowledge as a society." With this increase in knowledge, according to Clay, "humanity will find within itself an ability to develop peacefully and prosperously at a pace we have never before experienced."[1]

Others have famously argued—through song more frequently than the written word—that love is what the world most needs. Hal David and Burt Bacharach told us in 1965, "What the world needs now is love, sweet love." The Beatles told us in 1967, "All you need is love." If we just loved one another, the notion goes, all would be well. The world would be made right.

The problem is, neither of these solutions actually works. The Western world in the early nineteenth century, perhaps more than any other culture in history, believed education was what the world needed most. It only took a couple of world wars for sensible people to realize this wouldn't do the trick. The reality of sinful humanity is that we can turn knowledge into a weapon just like anything else, and anyway, there will always be more to learn. In the words of Ecclesiastes, "as knowledge increases, grief increases" (1:18).

What about love? Can love do what knowledge cannot? In theory, this idea is more appealing to us. But in practice, this won't get the job done either. The problem is, different people love different things, and even within each person, our loves contradict one another.

I, for example, being a true Texan, love Tex-Mex. And you can't have good Tex-Mex without queso. I *love* queso. But I also love my family. I love my wife, my kids, and my friends. The reality is, at some point, these loves will contradict one another! If I eat queso at lunch and dinner every day, I'm going to have some seriously clogged arteries, and the time I get to spend with my loved ones will be cut short. I have to choose between my loves. We all do.

So "love, sweet love," apparently, is not "all you need." What, then, does the world need most?

The World Needs Difference Makers

The thing your neighborhood, your city, your country, and the world needs most is difference makers. The world needs millions and millions of people who say together:

> *I was made for more than watching. I have a history-changing, difference-making, life-giving, Spirit-empowered legacy to leave. Jesus, I ask you to work deeply in me and clearly through me as I pray, give, and go in your love. I am a difference maker. In Jesus' name. Amen.*

Perhaps the most well-known teaching of Jesus comes in the Sermon on the Mount. In the Gospel of Matthew, Jesus has been doing miracles and announcing the kingdom of God for four chapters. Then, in chapter five, he goes up on a mountain and begins to teach his hearers. He teaches them about the "blessed" life—the life that is consistent with the values of the coming kingdom.

What do people living this life look like? It's not what we may be inclined to think. When we think of the blessed life, we think of health, wealth, and success. But Jesus' version is a little different. "Blessed are the poor in spirit," he begins, "for the kingdom of heaven is theirs" (v. 3). He goes on . . .

- "Blessed are those who mourn" (v. 4).
- "Blessed are the humble" (v. 5).
- "Blessed are those who hunger and thirst for righteousness" (v. 6).
- "Blessed are the merciful" (v. 7).
- "Blessed are the pure in heart" (v. 8).
- "Blessed are the peacemakers" (v. 9).
- "Blessed are those who are persecuted because of righteousness" (v. 10).
- "You are blessed when they insult you and persecute you and falsely say every kind of evil against you because of me" (v. 11).

This, according to Jesus, is the good life! When we are shaped by Jesus and the values of his kingdom, this is the kind of life it produces. And a funny thing happens when a whole bunch of people, following Jesus together, embody these characteristics. They become really helpful to the world. Check out what Jesus says a few verses later:

"You are the salt of the earth. But if the salt should lose its taste, how can it be made salty? It's not longer good for anything but to be thrown out and trampled under people's feet.

"You are the light of the world. A city situated on a hill cannot be hidden. No one lights a lamp and puts it under a basket, but rather on a lampstand, and it gives light for all who are in the house. In the same way, let your light shine before others, so that they may see your good works and give glory to your Father in heaven." (Matt. 5:13–16)

What the world needs most, then, is not education or love—as good as those things are. What the world needs most is salt and light. Salt—to preserve what is good in the world and to add flavor to the mundane nature of life "under the sun." Light—to give sight to a spiritually blind world, to illuminate the darkness, to expose sin and evil.

The word translated *you* in the verses above is a plural form of the word. If you live in the South like me, you might say, "Y'all are the salt of the earth. Y'all are the light of the world." The point is, it requires the community. None of us can, by ourselves, be the salt and light we're called to be; it's only when we come together that we can be truly good for the world. All of this so that the world "may see your good works and give glory to your Father in heaven" (Matt. 5:16).

Did you notice that last line? Difference makers aren't about getting glory for themselves. They're about getting glory for God. And when we embody the values of the kingdom and live together on the same page, we become salt and light, we become good for the world, and God gets the glory.

On the Same Page

Have you ever seen a musical score? A musical score is a "notation, in manuscript or printed form, of a musical work . . . A full, or orchestral, score shows all the parts of a large work, with each part on separate staves in vertical alignment."[2] As a pastor, I'm around musicians all the time, but I'm not a very musical person, so bear with me. A friend of mine showed me an orchestral score a while back for a song called "Hallelujah la de Samonte." Let me tell you, my mind was *blown*.

You've got all these different parts—piccolo, flute, oboe, oboe number two, English horn—probably forty different parts. And if a single one of them gets off the score, it ruins the entire performance! Unless all the various instrumentalists are on the same page, all tracking together, the production is messed up and doesn't accomplish the goal.

We can think of the church in the same way. The apostle Paul describes the church as a body with various members, or body parts. "Now there are different gifts," he says, "but the same Spirit. There are different ministries, but the same Lord. And there are different activities, but the same God produces each gift in each person" (1 Cor. 12:4–6). All of these various members or parts of the body of Christ need to be doing their job, playing their part, tracking along with the score of the gospel, in order for us to have a maximum impact in the world.

If what the world needs most is difference makers— believers embodying the values of the kingdom of God and living together as salt and light—we can't get off the score and start doing our own thing! We can't be divided over petty issues. We can't get caught up fighting about unimportant things. And we can't disagree over the most important thing.

Jesus left his followers with one last command before he ascended into heaven: "Go, therefore, and make disciples of all nations, baptizing them in the name of the Father and of the Son and of the Holy Spirit, teaching them to observe everything I have commanded you" (Matt. 28:19–20). That's making a difference! And that's the main thing. If we want to be difference makers, we need to be on the same page, focused on the main thing.

How Do You See Yourself?

Stop
2-8-21

In order for you to be on this page, to have your heart and mind in the right place, to be a difference maker, you have to see yourself rightly. You need to get into your mind that *you* are a difference maker.

Some of you may be reading this right now and thinking, *I'm not a difference maker. I'm just a college student trying to pass enough classes to graduate. I'm just a stay-at-home mom trying to keep these three kids from tearing up the house. I'm just an accountant. I'm just a retired person. I'm just a barista.*

First things first: take the word *just* out of your vocabulary! You are not *just* anything. Whether you're a college student, a stay-at-home mom, an accountant, a retired person, a barista, or anything else, you have a divinely orchestrated vocation. You have God-given talents and skills, and you are at a God-ordained station in life. He has a purpose in having you where you are right now, doing what you're doing right now. He has you there to make a difference.

Don't see your life as just a series of boxes to check. You're not sleepwalking through the day simply trying to get all the errands done, trying to get all the widgets made. You are a difference maker. God put you here to make a difference. Whatever station you are at in life, that is your vocation. Whether you like it or not, God has placed you on earth and where you are for a reason. Acts 17:26 tells us, "he has made every nationality to live over the whole earth and has determined their appointed times and the boundaries of where they live." Why? Look at the next verses, "He did this so that they might seek God, and perhaps they might reach out and find him, though he is not far from each one of us. For in him we live and move and have our being" (Acts 17:27–28).

God Works Through God's Word

Now that you're seeing yourself rightly—as an agent sent from God to make a difference in a broken world— we need to answer another question: *How can we make a difference?* The most fundamental answer to that question is this: God is the one who makes the difference. He is the ultimate difference maker.

Our God is Father, Son, and Holy Spirit—three-in-one. The theological term used to describe him is *Trinity*. And this triune God has been making a difference for all of history.

The Bible tells us that God created everything by his word. He spoke the universe into existence (Genesis 1). He called together his people, Israel, and ruled them by his word, the Law (Exodus 20). He holds all things together in Jesus, who is also called the Word (Col. 1:17; John 1:1).

God has always worked through his word, and now he has left his people with a Word: the Bible. The Bible "is inspired by God and is profitable for teaching, for rebuking, for correcting, for training in righteousness" (2 Tim. 3:16). God has given us, through his Word, "everything required for life and godliness" (2 Pet. 1:3). The psalmist says this about God's Word:

> The instruction of the LORD is perfect,
>   renewing one's life;
> the testimony of the LORD is trustworthy,
>   making the inexperienced wise.
> The precepts of the LORD are right, mak-
>   ing the heart glad;
> the command of the LORD is radiant,
>   making the eyes light up.
> The fear of the LORD is pure, enduring
>   forever;
> the ordinances of the LORD are reliable
>   and altogether righteous.

> They are more desirable than gold—than
>   an abundance of pure gold;
> and sweeter than honey dripping from a
>   honeycomb.
> In addition, your servant is warned by
>   them,
> and in keeping them there is an abundant
>   reward. (Ps. 19:7–11)

For us to be difference makers, first and foremost we have to get this. We have to understand and believe that the power to make a difference is not found in us; it's found in God. He is making a difference through his Word, and he will continue to do so. If we try to take matters into our own hands, speaking on our own authority rather than on God's, we will fail to make a difference.

So what should we do? We should read God's Word. We should submit to it. We should believe it. We should memorize it. We should meditate on it. We should come to know it so well that it permeates our hearts and minds, finds its way into our conversations, forms the content of our prayers. We should start with the Word and say to the Lord, "Father, confirm your Word with your Holy Spirit. Confirm your Word with your people. Give us wise counsel from your Word to go forward. Help us, through your Word, to be difference makers."

In our attempts to leave a "history-changing, differ-ence-making, life-giving, Spirit-empowered" legacy, we must start here. If we don't have the Word of God, we have nothing, and our attempts to make a difference will end in complete failure.

God Works through God's People

The amazing thing for us is, once we get God's Word into our hearts, God uses us to accomplish his plans and purposes.

Do you realize that God doesn't *need* us? Not in the slightest. He's the God of the universe! He had everything he could ever want in and of himself before he created the world. But create the world he did. And he created us in his image. He's invited us not only to share in fellowship with him, but to share in his mission.

One theologian looks at this reality as "God's relent-less commitment to work through seriously messed up people."[3] He's absolutely right! God doesn't need us, and he could accomplish his plans much faster and much less painfully without us. But in his grace, he has decided to use us. But we have to decide to be used.

Imagine the plans and purposes of God as a rushing river with a steep bank to one side. If you sit on the bank, you're not going to stop the river. You can root it on from the sidelines or you can hope and wish for it to stop, but it's just going to keep on rushing by. God's going to make a difference in the world, whether or not you want him to, and whether or not you participate.

But you have another option. Instead of watching the waters rush by, you can jump in. You can participate. You can experience the plan and the mission of God. God will work through you. He will use you, he will use us, his people, to make a difference in the world.

This is what the world needs most. Go get an education. School is good. Learning is good. It's a way we can know more about God and the world he has created, and knowledge rightly used will help serve people. And love. Love as hard as you can. Love your neighbors. Love your family. Love your enemies. But neither of these things by themselves—and certainly not on society's terms—are what the world needs most.

What the world needs most is difference makers. God is working in the world through his Word, and he's working through his people. He always has. When we jump into the rushing river of his work, embracing the values of his kingdom, we will be *good* for the world. We will be salt and light. We will be difference makers.

CHAPTER 3

The Man on the Mat and a Few Moms

We said in the last chapter that God works through his Word and through his people. Remember, God doesn't need us, but he graciously invites us to be a part of what he's doing in the world.

The amazing thing about the Bible and the history of God's people is that God seems to have this strange habit of using the most unlikely people to be difference makers. They're not the people you expect to make a difference. They're not people who have it all together. They're messy, broken people. They're sinful people. They're people with the odds stacked against them. They're people, well, like you and me.

This is exactly what the apostle Paul talked about in 2 Corinthians. He was an unlikely candidate to be a difference maker. Before his conversion to Christ, he persecuted the church! And even after he became a Christian, he had weaknesses. He referred to one of them as a "thorn in the flesh." Look at what he says:

> So that I would not exalt myself, a thorn in the flesh was given to me, a messenger of Satan to torment me so that I would not exalt myself. Concerning this, I pleaded with the Lord three times that it would leave me. But he said to me, "My grace is sufficient for you, for my power is perfected in weakness." (2 Cor. 12:7–9)

Even the apostle Paul had weaknesses, but God uses people with obvious weaknesses. Why? So that it can be clear that God is the one doing the work. His power is perfected in weakness. When it's clear that we are too weak and powerless to make such an amazing difference, it also becomes clear that God is the one making the difference.

The Bible is filled with stories like that, so that's where we're going now. We're going to look, in each chapter, at difference makers from the Bible. We'll look at the Old Testament and the New Testament and see these unlikely difference makers God used to accomplish his plan and purposes in the world. And we'll start with one of the most unlikely of the bunch: a paralyzed man.

The Man and His Friends

One of the most remarkable miracles Jesus performed early in his ministry is recorded in Matthew 9:1–8, Mark 2:1–12, and Luke 5:17–26. I encourage you to read the story now in one or all of these three Gospels.

Jesus is doing ministry in Capernaum, and some guys bring to him a paralytic lying on a mat. In Mark, we see that the man's friends cut a hole in the roof of the house Jesus is in and lowers their friend down into the house. Jesus sees their great faith and heals the man. But first, he does something else even more important: he tells the man his sins are forgiven.

This makes the religious leaders very angry. They think Jesus is blaspheming, as he claims authority—the authority to forgive sins. That power belongs to God and God alone. But, of course, this forgiveness and the subsequent healing made the man very excited. I imagine him skipping away carrying his mat—maybe even dumping it in a pile of garbage somewhere. After all, he didn't need that mat anymore; he had been healed!

And when the crowds saw what happened, they were astounded. They were amazed at the authority of Jesus—to forgive sins and to heal. And they gave glory to God.

Difference Making Starts with the Heart

We can learn much from this story about difference makers. The first and most obvious thing we see is what we already said above—that God uses the most unlikely of people as difference makers. A guy paralyzed, presumably from the neck down, unable to move himself from place to place, in an age with no wheelchairs or modern technology to help overcome such difficulties? Surely he's not a likely candidate to be a difference maker. But Jesus chooses and uses the weak in order to display his strength and power.

We tend to focus on the weakness of this man's body, but Jesus first noticed another weakness—a weakness of heart. Jesus knew what we need to understand: difference making starts with the heart. As long as this man had a heart that was opposed to God—a sinful heart, a hard heart—he wouldn't be a difference maker. So before Jesus says, "Get up and take your mat and walk out of here"— that's coming later—he says, "Your sins are forgiven."

And this statement by Jesus infuriated those who heard it. Matthew 9:3 says, "At this, some of the scribes said to themselves, 'He's blaspheming!'" They were angry because, in claiming to forgive this man's sins, Jesus was making another claim, a more fundamental claim, a more disruptive claim: he was claiming to be God.

The Pharisees and scribes knew, just like Jesus knew, that the only one who can forgive sins is God. God alone is the judge of all people. When we sin, we sin against him (Ps. 51:4). So by claiming to forgive this man's sin, Jesus was saying, "I am God in the flesh." This was a statement of deity. And it freaked people out.

This wasn't only a claim about who Jesus was; it was a claim about who the paralyzed man was. The man was a sinner. Because of his sin, he wasn't in right relationship with God. Sin is always the problem; being rightly related with God is always the answer. The Bible tells us that "all have sinned and fall short of the glory of God," and "the wages of sin is death" (Rom. 3:23; 6:23). It tells us we all come into this world "dead in [our] trespasses and sins . . . children under wrath" (Eph. 2:1, 3). But there is good news! God doesn't want to leave us that way. Jesus came to earth, lived the life we failed to live, died the death we deserved to die, and was raised from the grave in order to give us life. Let's listen to Jesus tell us this in his own words:

> "For God loved the world in this way: He gave his one and only Son, so that everyone who believes in him will not perish but have eternal life. For God did not send his Son into the world to condemn the world, but to save the world through him.

Anyone who believes in him is not condemned, but anyone who does not believe
is already condemned, because he has not
believed in the name of the one and only
Son of God." (John 3:16–18)

Have you believed in Jesus? Do you trust that he
died on the cross, taking the punishment for sin that we
deserved? God's Word tells us that if we confess that
Jesus is Lord and believe that God raised him from the
dead, we will be saved (Rom. 10:9). When this happens,
God removes our hard hearts and gives us soft hearts,
receptive to his leading (Ezek. 36:26). When we have these
soft hearts, we're ready to follow Jesus into the world.
We're ready to be difference makers.

Difference Makers Have Courage

Jesus says something interesting to this paralyzed
man during this miracle. Look at verse two of Matthew 9:
"Have courage, son, your sins are forgiven." We see here
that if we want to be difference makers, we must have
courage.

Jesus wanted the man on the mat to have courage. He
wanted him to be of good cheer. He wanted him to stand
up and go for it, to be bold.

This kind of courage is hard to come by in our world. To be honest, we live in a society where there's a lot of things to fear. Not long ago, I took my kids to go see a movie, and on the way out, my wife said, "Have fun at the move. Be safe." *Be safe.* That struck me in a new way. We can't even go to the movies anymore without having to think about being safe.

And that's the case in the United States, one of the safest countries in the world. While we live with the seemingly constant threat of mass shootings or terrorism, the list of things we have to be afraid of pales in comparison with billions of people in different parts of the world.

If we want to be difference makers in a world like this, we have to keep moving in spite of our fears. We have to have courage. Courage isn't the absence of fear; it's the absence of self. To move forward with courage doesn't mean you're not afraid of anything; it means your main focus is on God and others, not yourself, so you can do what you know you're called to do even if it puts you at risk.

My wife, Kelly, was invited to a women's prayer group on Tuesday nights after these moms got the little ones to bed. Like all difference-making endeavors, it began with a burden. One of the participants, Leigh, opened her home for a prayer meeting after deciding something had to be done about human trafficking. How could she hear the stats declared at a conference she attended and go back to life as usual? But at the same time, how is a stay-at-home mom of three going to battle such a powerful and ruthless industry?

This group of ladies prayed prayers of power. This wasn't a *pray a bit then eat some brownies* church group. As they courageously prayed, God moved. This difference-making thing requires the audacity to say, "Not in our city. God, we are calling on you." Leigh opened her home, the ladies opened their hearts, and God opened the heavens. I remember reading articles in the *Houston Chronicle* about brothels being raided and enslaved women being rescued. I would call out to Kelly, "God is answering your prayers, and it is documented in the newspaper!" How amazing to see real-time change in the third largest city in the United States coming from the valor of sweet, kind, and shaking-the-gates-of-hell church ladies.

The story doesn't end there. With the encouragement of her husband and friends, Leigh gallantly helped start the "Freedom Church Alliance"[1] that connects churches together to fight human trafficking in Houston. They now have an office and staff members who are a resource for the City of Houston, law enforcement, and several anti-trafficking organizations. They fund strategic projects and developed a tool kit called "The Go Box" to empower everyday people to fight trafficking. They are making a huge difference.

What a difference-making story only God could write. A sweet stay-at-home mom of three along with prayerful women decides to stand up against organized evil AND is seeing victories!

How did this happen? Courage, faith, consistency, and prayer. Not muscle, brawn, or personality. "'Not by strength or by might, but by my Spirit,' says the LORD . . ." (Zech. 4:6). With ladies praying, leaders leading, and God moving . . . look out, traffickers! Look out, world! Where is God calling you to have more courage than you do? Just take the next step.[2]

Now let's turn our attention back to the man on the mat. Think about the fear in his mind when Jesus told him, "Get up and walk." Who knows how long it had been since this guy was on his feet? It's possible he was born this way. And Jesus just looks him in the eye and calmly says, "Get up and walk."

Is this a joke? Is somebody messing with him? Are his friends trying to trick him or embarrass him? Imagine the shame and the ridicule if Jesus tells him to get up and he still can't move.

Not only did getting up require courage, it required the man, in a sense, to get out of his comfort zone. Now, you might not get this at first. You might think, *Are you kidding me? Get out of his comfort zone? The guy hasn't walked in years; why wouldn't he want to get up immediately?* But maybe he had grown comfortable—emotionally, relationally, mentally—on his mat. Apparently he had good friends who were taking care of him. Not much was required of him. Maybe he had grown accustomed to the status quo.

Are you accustomed to the status quo in your life? Are you comfortable not making a difference? Have you grown to enjoy sitting on the sidelines? Many of us grow into this sort of lazy Christianity. We know we're going to heaven when we die, so we're set, right? Why get out of our comfort zone? But we should know this is not the way we're made to live. Just like this man was created to walk and skip and run and jump and clap his hands and hug and high-five, we were created to get in the game, to work, to serve, to sacrifice, and to love people with everything we have. It may be uncomfortable, and it certainly requires courage, but it's what you were made for. You can't make a difference on the sidelines.

Difference Makers Point to Their Savior

There's one more thing the man on the mat teaches us about being a difference maker. Look with me at Matthew 9:7–8: "So he got up and went home. When the crowds saw this, they were awestruck and gave glory to God, who had given such authority to men."

Capernaum was a decent-sized town for its day, but not large by any means. It had somewhere in the neighborhood of fifteen hundred citizens during the life of Jesus.[3] It was certainly small enough that people around town would have been familiar with one another, would have known what family somebody came from, and certainly would have been familiar with those who stood out in society, like this paralyzed man. My wife is from Comfort, Texas—which boasts twelve hundred people—and she has assured me word travels fast in these dots on the map. So when he takes off running and celebrating with his mat, this is the biggest news all week. People recognize him, so naturally, they're amazed. *It's that paralyzed guy! He's not paralyzed anymore!*

And what is the result? Look back up to verse 8. To whom did the people give glory? Not to the man who was healed. No way. They gave glory to God.

Here's the thing about difference makers. Difference makers shine with their Savior, not their success.

The man on the mat (who's now just the man *with* the mat) doesn't go around making a big show of himself. Matthew 9 doesn't say everyone stood around and applauded him for learning how to walk and jump and dance. They didn't form a circle and start clapping for him, cheering him on. They gave glory to God, who in his Son, Jesus, healed the man. The people were awed, not by the difference maker himself, but by the one who healed him.

When people think of difference makers, we tend to think of successful people. Powerful politicians. Popular musicians. Athletes with max contracts. Fortune 500 CEOs. They can definitely be used by God in huge ways. But, at times, this kind of difference making is focused on the self, and it doesn't last. When we try to make a difference by being successful for our glory, we rob God of his glory, and we put our efforts toward something that may make a difference for a little while, but isn't eternal. Ecclesiastes says, "I hated all my work that I labored at under the sun because I must leave it to the one who comes after me. And who knows whether he will be wise or a fool?" (2:18–19). In other words, even if you do something that makes a difference for your whole life, the person who comes after you could ruin it!

But that's not so when we make a difference with Jesus. It's not so when the gospel is what drives the difference. When God, through his Word and through his people, is changing hearts and lives.

That's why God so often uses seemingly unsuccessful people as difference makers. It's not always the celebrity athlete or musician, it's not the most attractive or wealthy person; it's weak, unimpressive people, like all of us. It's just men and women who hear the Lord and do something about it. God's power is made perfect in our weakness. So when God uses us to make a difference, it's very clear who's doing the heavy lifting. And he's the one who gets the glory.

Pastor Thomas

When people are changed at the heart level and God gives them courage, they become difference makers. They live on purpose, and in their intentionality, God does things through them that make it clear that God is the one at work, and he gets all the glory. I want to tell you a story about a friend of mine who is one such difference maker.

A member of the church I pastor was on a mission trip in Africa. On one of the days while he was there, some of the group members went on a safari—a sort of fun day in the middle of a challenging, difficult week. His safari guide's name was Thomas.

This friend of mine realized during the safari that Thomas was not a believer in Jesus. But my friend knew the good news that Jesus didn't come to condemn the world, but to save the world, and that those who believe in Jesus will have eternal life.

So my friend told Thomas the good news. He started with the heart. He had courage. He was a difference maker. He allowed himself to be used by God to speak the truth of the gospel to Thomas, and Thomas believed. He responded in faith and received Christ.

Thomas realized not long after that he had a call on his life. So he, like my friend, decided to be a difference maker. He wasn't going to sit on the sidelines and watch his friends and family stumble through life in the darkness. So he started sharing the gospel. He led half of his tribe to Christ. Next thing you know, Thomas the unbelieving safari guide has turned into Pastor Thomas, shepherding a growing church of more than two hundred!

Pastor Thomas's church was also helping with a school in the tribe, where more than three hundred children attended. The local government saw the good work the school was doing, and decided to build another school. Now, our church gets to partner with that church and the schools to provide textbooks. Now, because of our working relationship with the tribe and the tribe's good relationship with the government, our church has been able to assist in building water wells so the tribe can have access to clean and healthy water. People are being saved spiritually with the good news of Jesus and physically with schools and textbooks and clean water! And why? Because one guy decided to be a difference maker.

So what about you? Are you ready to get off the sidelines? Are you ready to be like the man on the mat? Have the courage of Leigh and the ladies? To learn from my friend who shared the gospel with Thomas? To follow the example of Pastor Thomas? If so, say yes, start something, join something, sign up, share, serve . . . make a difference!

> *I was made for more than watching. I have a history-changing, difference-making, life-giving, Spirit-empowered legacy to leave. Jesus, I ask you to work deeply in me and clearly through me as I pray, give, and go in your love. I am a difference maker. In Jesus' name. Amen.*

CHAPTER 4

Dinner with Linebackers and Liars

As I sat down at the table it was easy to figure out who was not like the others. Before I spoke at the Texas A&M football chapel, I found myself sitting with the linebackers for Saturday's game. My football career consisted of the eighth grade bench and some college intermurals, and here I sat with the gladiators of the gridiron. Their position coach was a believer and acquaintance of mine, so he made the introductions around the table and my 5'7" frame was seated with giants.

It was fun to watch them consume days' worth of food on one plate and also to realize they were college kids like any others, just twice as big. But I also recognized I was the only one in the room who wasn't on the team. They were different in size and skill, and all wearing the same warm-ups. I felt a strange combination of being out of place and welcomed. Matthew possibly felt the same way when Jesus showed up for dinner. Why would the Messiah eat with people in a mess of sin? Yet it felt so right.

We're picking back up in Matthew 9, immediately following the story of the man on the mat. In verses 10–13, we read a story about Jesus at dinner. In the verse right before that, we hear about a man named Matthew—the author of this Gospel. Jesus calls Matthew, who we're told here is "sitting at the tax booth" (v. 9 ESV), to follow him, and Matthew does. Then the story quickly shifts to a different scene: Jesus is in his house eating dinner. And who is he eating with? A motley crew. Tax collectors, sinners, and Pharisees. It's more unexpected than a preacher in a room of football players.

Dinner, Tax Collectors, and Pharisees

For us to grasp the significance of what's going on here, there are some cultural elements we need to understand. What was the significance of dinner in Jesus' day? What's up with tax collectors? Why didn't the Pharisees like them? What is a Pharisee anyway? Once we've considered these things, we'll learn from Jesus that difference makers dine in diversity while speaking with clarity.

Dinner

Food is a big deal in American culture. It's really a big deal in Texan culture. We love our food—especially barbecue. You really haven't had brisket unless you've had it in Texas.

We don't just love to eat our food; we love to look at it, to take pictures of it, and to see pictures of the food other people are eating. Just consider the fact that in 2016, *Business Insider* ran an article ranking the top fifty best food bloggers on Instagram.[1] (If you're interested, their top-ranked account, at the time of this writing, boasts more than six million followers.)

Food was a big deal in Jesus' culture too, although for different reasons. Needless to say, Jesus wasn't taking pictures of his food and posting it on Instagram. The point of dinner wasn't about getting a bunch of likes or even making the meal look really pretty. No, in Jesus' day and age, to eat a meal with another person was to make a statement of fellowship. It was to associate in an intimate way with another person.

One scholar puts it this way: "Table fellowship in Judaism was more than food. . . . In the ancient world, to share the table with another person was making a social statement about yourself and about your guest."[2] So by eating a meal with tax collectors and sinners (v. 10), Jesus was making a radical public statement—he was destroying the social barriers that stood between himself, a God-fearing Jew, and tax collectors.

But what's the big deal about the tax collectors? That is the next cultural element we need to understand if we're going to grasp the significance of this story.

Tax Collectors

Tax collectors in Jesus' day were perhaps the most hated, reviled people in Jewish society. Now, in our day and age, we're not big fans of tax collectors either. We know they've got a job to do and that's good and we appreciate that. But they take our money! It's not like anybody's just really in love with the IRS, inviting the IRS over for dinner every weekend. Can you imagine? "Here, take a look at my W-2s and make sure everything's in good shape."

But in Jesus' day, tax collectors were much more hated and reviled than that. The Roman Empire was the world superpower during Jesus' life, and they had some interesting practices as they took over the majority of the known world. One of these practices was to employ tax collectors from the people they conquered. So, when the Romans conquered the Jews, they hired Jewish tax collectors.

For the Jews, this was grievous treachery. The Jews were the people of God. He was their one and only God. His promise to them, dating all the way back to Abraham in Genesis 12, was that he would give them a land and prosperity. He promised them in 2 Samuel 7 that there would be a king from the offspring of David forever and ever. But now, they've been partially displaced from the land—many of them were scattered abroad—and there's a foreign king over them who doesn't fear or worship God and doesn't respect them. Some kings thought they were gods. So what do the tax collectors do? They sell out. Tax collectors looked at the situation and saw a business opportunity—an opportunity to get rich by partaking in the oppression of their own people. They abandoned their fellow Israelites, got in league with the oppressive Roman Empire, participated in keeping the Jews underfoot, *and* got rich by skimming a little off the top, to boot.

Needless to say, they were the worst of the worst. They were despised.

But Jesus, in verse 9, calls one of these scoundrels to be his disciple. "Matthew," he says, "leave your tax booth and follow me." And Matthew does just that.

Apparently, Matthew was like Pastor Thomas, who went and invited all of the people in his tribe and his coworkers to meet Jesus for dinner at his house, because next thing we know, Jesus is sitting at the dinner table sharing a meal with tax collectors.

So let's recap. To share a meal in Jesus' culture was to communicate social equality and intimacy. The tax collectors were the most hated, reviled sinners in society. And Jesus was sharing a meal with tax collectors. Now we turn to our third and final cultural element.

Pharisees

If you've been around the church for a while, you probably think you've got the Pharisees figured out. They're bullies. They were arrogant, stuck-up know-it-alls who were always clashing with Jesus because they were so self-righteous. But it's important to know that this isn't at all how Pharisees were thought of in their day. New Testament scholar Mark Strauss says:

> Today the term Pharisee is often equated with hypocrisy and a legalistic spirit, but this would not have been the view of most people in first-century Israel, who generally respected the Pharisees for their piety and devotion to the law. Indeed, the Pharisees' fundamental goal was a noble one: to maintain a life of purity and obedience to God's law.[3]

However bad the tax collectors were thought to be in Jesus' day, the Pharisees were thought to be that good. Some may have had good intentions. They were so zealous about obeying God's law that they didn't even want to get close to breaking it. So they built a hedge around it—a whole bunch of rules that would prevent them from even coming close to breaking the Law. This is what Jesus referred to as their "tradition."

As you can imagine, while the tax collectors were seen as super unspiritual, the Pharisees were seen as super spiritual. They were so spiritual that they defined to a T, even discerning which types of knots were and weren't acceptable to tie on the Sabbath.

So what, then, was so wrong with the Pharisees? Why did they butt heads with Jesus so often? Jesus' problem wasn't so much that the Pharisees wanted to keep the Law—his problem was that they wanted to do all the right things, but for all the wrong reasons. So he calls them hypocrites. Later in Matthew, he says, "Woe to you, scribes and Pharisees, hypocrites! You are like white-washed tombs, which appear beautiful on the outside, but inside are full of the bones of the dead and every kind of impurity" (23:27). Strong words here from Jesus! His problem with the Pharisees was that they followed the Law not to please God, but to impress people (Matt. 6:1, 5, 16). And in their attempts to impress people, they placed their tradition above God's law, and ended up breaking the most important parts of it, like love and mercy (Matt. 15:3–9).

Diversity and Clarity

Now that we have a hold on some of the cultural elements at play in Matthew 9, let's return to the story. Jesus invites Matthew, a tax collector, to follow him, and Matthew does. Immediately, Jesus is seen eating dinner with tax collectors and sinners. It's unclear here whether Pharisees were also invited to the dinner. They probably weren't, but rather were watching. Plus, from what we know about Pharisees, they likely wouldn't have eaten dinner even in the presence of the tax collectors.

But we know that elsewhere in the Bible Jesus did eat with Pharisees. A similar story is told in Luke 7. Jesus is eating dinner at a Pharisee's house and a "sinful woman"—probably a prostitute—just barges right into the house. She starts crying all over Jesus, kissing his feet, essentially worshiping him in the house of the Pharisee. The Pharisees are indignant, wondering why Jesus keeps company with such sinners, and in Matthew 9, they have the same attitude. "Why," they ask his disciples, "does your teacher eat with tax collectors and sinners?" (Matt. 9:11).

This is where we learn an essential lesson from Jesus about being a difference maker. Jesus, the ultimate difference maker, dined in diversity while speaking with clarity.

Jesus Dined in Diversity

Dining in Jesus' day was a sign of intimate fellowship, and here, he's dining with the people who no one would have expected a rabbi like him to dine with. In Luke 7, the other story we mentioned, he's dining with people who we, who have such a bad taste in our mouths about Pharisees, would never expect a radical like him to dine with. But Jesus came for all kinds of people. He welcomed people of diversity—the apparently self-righteous and the obviously sinful, the Jew and the Gentile, men and women, adults and little children. In every case, Jesus spent time with the elite of the day *and* the outcast of the day. Blind people, paralyzed people, lepers, impoverished people—all thought to be under the wrath of God. Tax collectors, Gentiles, women, and little children—all thought to be unimportant and insignificant in the eyes of God. And Jesus spent time with them all.

Diversity is a buzzword in our culture. Talking about diversity in the public square will win you points. And sadly, the church has lagged behind in many ways. Martin Luther King Jr. famously said, "It is appalling that the most segregated hour of Christian America is eleven o'clock on Sunday morning." Tragically, this sort of division is still apparent in our churches and at our dinner tables.

King was talking specifically about racial or ethnic division, and he was right—this sort of division is appalling. And there are other sorts of division. We divide along lines of race, yes, and also along lines of socioeconomic status and income levels, cultural preferences and backgrounds, political persuasion, and even which sports team to root for! James Taranto in June of 2017 wrote in the opening sentence of a *Wall Street Journal* article, "If there's one thing Americans of all political stripes can agree on, it's that the country is divided—bitterly, dangerously, perhaps irreconcilably riven."[4] Is he wrong?

In the midst of this division, Christians, of all people, ought to pursue radical hospitality and love of neighbor that just doesn't make sense if Jesus is still in the grave. Jesus' day was no less divided than ours in terms of class, race, gender, and social status, yet he obliterated those boundaries by dining in diversity. Are you willing to do the same? To be a difference maker, I believe we must. I believe our dinner tables, Saturday afternoon cups of coffee, birthday parties, contact lists, and our churches all must massively increase in diversity for us to make the difference that Jesus is calling us to make.

Not only that, but we must develop relationships with people whose lifestyles are much different than ours. We're not only seeking diversity racially, socially, or socioeconomically; to be a difference maker means to spend time with sinners. To dine with people who are far from God. That's what Jesus did, and that's what we're called to do.

There's another thing to note here before we move on. Maybe you're reading this right now thinking, *I don't need to dine with tax collectors . . . I am a tax collector.* You may think you're such a bad sinner that even Jesus wouldn't want to dine with you. And maybe Christians have basically told you that. If that's you, I want you to hear this loud and clear: this passage of Scripture shows that no one, *no one* is outside the pursuit of Jesus Christ. He loves you, he came not to condemn you but to save you, and he wants to be in relationship with you. He wants to dine with you. Take him up on his offer.

Jesus Spoke with Clarity

The second lesson Jesus teaches us about being a difference maker here is that we must speak with clarity. Jesus spent a lot of time around tax collectors and sinners. He spoke at one point with an adulterous woman (John 4). He was way more radical in his relationships that most of us want to be, than most of us have been told to be, as Christians. But as close as Jesus got in relationship and proximity to sinners, he never once condoned their sinful behavior or do what we so often do, passively agree.

Jesus does an amazing tightrope walk in his ministry. Some of us are either verbally or mentally condemning to sinners. I have fallen into the trap of being so aggravated with how so-and-so is messing up society for me and my future grandkids. It's a difficult place to stand for truth, even vote for truth, while loving the lobbyist on the other side. God's calling us to do something far more difficult than obnoxiously picket, parade, and shout at people with blow horns. He's calling us to love well and reach out.

In a reaction to our polarizing world some of us are so afraid we'll appear to be condemning people that we end up going along with sinful behavior. It's like we want so badly to be accepted by the tax collectors of our day that we end up saying, either with words or with our actions, "No, I think it's great that you're a tax collector. Ripping people off is just part of the job." But Jesus doesn't do that. He never once condones sinful behavior. He didn't condone the sinful behavior of the adulterous woman in John 4. He forgave the woman in Luke 7 of her sins. He called Matthew away from the toll booth in Matthew 9. In every case, we see Jesus moving into relationship, not condemning but also not condoning. Rather, he's calling people out of their lives of sin into a life of following him. It's a tough balance in our parenting, friendships, and workplaces.

But this is what difference makers must do. We must speak with clarity and love. Be encouraged; God will lead you. He will give you the right words that are laced with love, not forced with agenda. You are reading this book because you desire to love God and people more, so I know something about you—you want to turn people to Jesus, not away. God knows your heart. You can trust him to strike the right balance in your "meal time" conversations.

Here's the key to being able to dine in diversity while speaking with clarity. Who else is in the picture in Matthew 9:9–13? Jesus' disciples. His inner circle. The core of his friends.

Who is the core of your social group? Are they encouragers to your spiritual journey? First Corinthians 15:33 says, "Do not be deceived: 'Bad company corrupts good morals.'" If your core group of friends is walking in spiritual shadows or darkness instead of the light, you will be pulled down more than they are pulled up. Undoubtedly, difference makers don't live in a bubble but a balance. We need to be connected with spiritual encouragers and reach out in ministry to those that are struggling.

Why Jesus Came, Why We Go

Jesus said something interesting here at the end of this conversation. In response to the Pharisees' question to the disciples about why he was eating with tax collectors and sinners, Jesus said this:

> "It is not those who are well who need a
> doctor, but those who are sick. Go and

learn what this means: I desire mercy and not sacrifice. For I didn't come to call the righteous, but sinners." (Matt. 9:12–13)

This is the motivation for why Jesus dined in diversity and spoke with clarity. He had a mission. He came to earth for a reason—to heal the spiritually sick, to call sinners into a life of following him. Jesus had a great clarity of identity. He knew who he was (is) and what his purpose was on earth. He came to reach out to and care for the sinner, to make a difference in the lives of sinners.

The Pharisees had their own mission. They were trying to keep the Law perfectly. They were very sacrificial—always showing off how much they sacrificed. But Jesus in a sense was saying to them, "Don't you get that the most important part of the Law isn't about sacrifice? It's about mercy. I don't care nearly as much about the sacrifices you make; I want you to go have mercy on somebody."

The Pharisees thought they were righteous. See, Jesus is being kind of ironic or sarcastic here. "I didn't come to call the righteous," he says, and I can imagine him following it up with, "since you guys think you're so righteous." But he came to call sinners and people who knew they were sinners. He didn't condone the sin of the tax collectors. He came to call them out of it.

And that's exactly what Jesus did in this passage. He had mercy. He mercifully ate dinner with people who were far from God. He made a public statement of intimate friendship and fellowship with the most reviled sinners. He made crystal clear what his mission was, why he came.

I have dined at the White House and also with those without any home. Interstate 10 that runs across the United States goes right by the Loop campus of our church. I can see cars passing from my office window. An interstate means bridges, and in an urban environment, bridges often mean people living underneath. I have become friends with a few of these people. Melissa lived under a bridge by our church and would come on Sundays at times. It was always fun for me to be turning at the light, roll down my window, and call out, "Hey, Melissa, have a great day." She would wave and yell back, "You, too, Pastor Gregg!"

One day on my way home, I pulled up to the light and Melissa was there with a homeless man I hadn't met. I asked if they were hungry, and they send yes. I told them to jump in and took them to McDonald's.

Excited as kids, they jumped in and off we went. Melissa leaned between the front seats with me driving and a twenty-ish-year-old guy riding shotgun. Just one big happy family. We didn't look good or smell good rolling up to the McDonald's counter, but who cares! Once our order arrived, I found myself sharing French fries and sharing the gospel. I giggled to myself thinking as people glanced over at our booth with me dressed in a crisply starched shirt and flat fronts and my friends in the weathered thrift store fashion line. But I'm not living for other's glances; I'm living for God's eyes. So . . . I'm going to dine in diversity and also speak with clarity. What a joy to have both the White House and McDonald's in my life!

And the same reason Jesus came is the reason we go. The reason we go to our neighbors. To our family members who are far from God. Or maybe to the other side of the world. Or under a bridge.

Where is God calling you to make a difference? He's calling you to go somewhere, even if it's just to the house next door. He's calling you to get off the sideline, to take the gospel to those who need to hear it. It's not the healthy who need a doctor, but the sick. Jesus is calling us to go, not to the "righteous," but to the lost. Some of those are filthy rich and some are just filthy. Let's love both enough to have a meal together. Jesus is calling us to say:

> *I was made for more than watching. I have a history-changing, difference-making, life-giving, Spirit-empowered legacy to leave. Jesus, I ask you to work deeply in me and clearly through me as I pray, give, and go in your love. I am a difference maker. In Jesus' name. Amen.*

CHAPTER 5

The Disposition of a Difference Maker

Niagara Falls is a sight like no other. A hundred and eighty feet of countless gallons of falling water making a roar and spraying mist to the sky will stop you in your tracks. But before you get to the falls, it is for the most part a peaceful river filled with boaters. Plenty beautiful and calming until you get to a certain sign posted just before the Welland River merges with the Niagara River. The sign simply asks two questions:

1. Do you have an anchor?
2. Do you know how to use it?

Great questions for life. Our anchor is our identity in Christ, and we must learn to use it.[1]

What Is Your Identity?

Who are you?

There are many ways to answer this question. You generally start with your name, first and last—an identity that was given to you by your parents. This is where many of us find our identity—in our families of origin, in our spouses, or in our children.

Many others of us find our identity in what we do. *What do you do, Gregg? I'm a pastor.* Notice the shift in language—the question was what do you *do*? The answer was I *am*. And that's not just true of pastors. You might say, *I'm a mom. I'm a college student. I'm an accountant. I'm a plumber. I'm a doctor.* Certainly in American culture, many of us find our identity in what we do.

Our society has much to say about identity. "What you feel is what you are, and what you are is beautiful," we say.[2] In other words, the thing that's most fundamental about you is whatever you feel. Your deepest longings, desires, and emotions are not just a part of your identity; they *are* your identity. That's what our culture tells us.

But can any of these identities really hold up? What happens when any or all of these things are taken away from us? When we lose the family that brought us into this world, or the family we created with a beloved spouse? When we lose the job we went to school and grad school and worked overtime to get? When the pursuit of fulfillment and pleasure leaves us empty and wanting?

Timothy Keller argues that the modern conception of identity is crushing. "It must base itself on success or achievement or some human love relationship, and if any of these things is jeopardized or lost, you lose your very identity."[3] So what can we do? What happens when we lose all that we look to for our identity? Is there any sense of self that can withstand suffering and loss?

Identity in Exile

The people of God lost everything. Let's do a little history lesson of the Old Testament. Around 2000 BC, God called a man named Abram to follow him. You can read about it in Genesis 12 and the following chapters. He entered into a covenant with Abram. God told Abram to follow him, and he made a promise to him:

> "Go out from your land, your relatives, and your father's house to the land that I will show you. I will make you into a great nation, I will bless you, I will make your name great, and you will be a blessing. I will bless those who bless you, I will curse anyone who treats you with contempt, and all the peoples on earth will be blessed through you." (Gen. 12:1–3)

God went on to promise Abram that his descendants would be more numerous than the stars, and that he would give them a land to inherit. He promised that he would be their God and they would be his people.

God changed Abram's name to Abraham, and at the ripe old ages of one hundred and ninety, respectively, Abraham and Sarah gave birth to their son, Isaac. After Isaac came Jacob, whose name was changed to Israel, and he had twelve sons, after whom were named the twelve tribes of Israel. During a famine, they were taken to Egypt by one of the brothers—Joseph, whom God had given a prominent position there. He protected them and kept them well fed and cared for during the famine.

Fast-forward about five hundred years, and we get to the book of the Bible called Exodus. We read there: "A new king, who did not know about Joseph, came to power in Egypt" (Exod. 1:8). This new king grew afraid of the Israelites because God was blessing them and multiplying them, so he enslaved them. But God acted in a mighty way to raise up a leader named Moses, and through Moses, he led his people out of slavery in Egypt and took them toward the land that he had promised Abraham.

But the Israelites were disobedient to God. They were stubborn and kept complaining about them, so he made them wander in the wilderness for forty years before he brought them into the Promised Land. Moses, the great prophet and leader, died without getting to see the Promised Land, and God raised up another leader after him—Joshua. Through Joshua, God led his people into the Promised Land.

But things went downhill from there. The Bible tells of generations of disobedience in the book of Judges. God had rescued his people from slavery, he had multiplied them as he promised Abraham he would, and then he had led them into the Promised Land, but they were hard-hearted and kept disobeying him. "In those days," says the last verse of Judges, "there was no king in Israel; everyone did whatever seemed right to him" (21:25).

The people complained to God because the nations around them had kings and they didn't have a king. They wanted to be like the other nations, even though God called them to be different and distinct from the surrounding nations. Nonetheless, he gave them what they wanted—kings. Around the year 1000 BC, you get the first three kings: Saul, David, and Solomon. David famously committed adultery with a woman named Bathsheba and then had her husband killed to cover it up . . . and he was the *best* king Israel ever had.

After Solomon, the kingdom was divided into two kingdoms—Israel in the north and Judah in the south. Things continued to spiral downhill as the people perpetually rejected God and worshiped false gods. God told the people before they ever entered the Promised Land that if they worshiped false gods and rejected him, they would be exiled from the Promised Land, but they ignored him. They hardened their hearts and continued in sin until God finally made good on his promise—he kicked them out of the Promised Land. In 586 BC, the people were exiled, taken captive, and purged from the land God had given to them.

Now imagine you're an Israelite. What do you base your entire identity in? Your ethnicity (Hebrew). The Law God has given you. The cultural distinctives in that Law. And the promise God gave you—the Promised Land.

Now imagine you're an exiled Israelite. You're still a Hebrew, but now you've been taken captive into a different culture. You're no longer allowed to obey fully the Law or the cultural distinctives of the Law. And you've been removed from the Promised Land. If you based your identity in those things, your identity was completely shattered. It was ruined. If the Israelites understood identity the same way we do, it would be safe to say their identity was completely shattered.

Your People, the Sheep of Your Pasture

Doubtless, many people did feel just like this, abandoned by God. Lost and purposeless in the world. But did they still have an identity? I think some of them—the ones who stayed sane and reminded themselves of the character of God—did.

Psalm 79 was written during the exile. The Babylonians have come. They've captured the Israelites. They've taken them away from the Promised Land. And here we get this psalm. I want to zoom in on one verse:

> Then we, *your people, the sheep of your pasture*, will thank you forever; we will declare your praise to generation after generation. (Ps. 79:13, emphasis added)

In this verse, I believe we see the disposition of a difference maker. This is a psalm of lament. The writer is crying out to God for deliverance, praying that God will rescue his people from exile. He trusts that God will do just that. But there's one thing he doesn't lose sight of, even in the midst of exile: "we, your people, the sheep of your pasture." Even in exile, even without any hope of a return to the Promised Land in sight, this psalmist knew who he was. He knew who the people of Israel were. They were God's people, the sheep of his pasture.

This book began with our city's journey through Hurricane Harvey. If there was a time that identity in the exterior was shaken in our city, that was it. Whether you had a mansion or a rental, three feet of water inside is the same punch in the gut. More than striking our monetary comforts, it was the emotional trauma of life being up-ended that really shook us. Those first weeks were so hard that we had to trust the Shepherd still held his sheep, because it didn't seem so.

When the rain began to crest the doorsteps of church members, I tried to call every one of them, but within hours I couldn't keep up. I wanted them to hear their pastoral shepherd's voice as life changed before their eyes. Those I called were so grateful, but the list grew too long to continue. Ultimately, more than seven hundred church members and twenty-three staff members lost their homes. One church member described his situation watching the water on the street invade the neighbor-hood's homes, in some cases up to five or more feet. Soggy carpet was turning into boat rescues. More than rescuing living rooms, we began rescuing lives.

Teams of church members organically organized and began canvassing neighborhoods to rescue anyone they could. One team headed to the house of John Bisagno, our pastor emeritus, to rescue him and his wife, Uldine. Both in their eighties and her in hospice care for brain cancer, I received a text message with a picture. The photo showed sweet Uldine, sopping wet from the rain with a blanket draped over her. She was in a boat with one of the rescue teams. The driver had one hand on the wheel and his other arm around her shoulders. His face and eyes were sternly set forward as if to say, "I got you and we are getting you outta here."

When I looked at the picture, my heart broke and tears fell. One, for the heroes commanding the boat, but more, for the Bisagnos. Lord, how can they serve you for eighty years and it end like this? Seventeen days later, Uldine died and they never returned to their home. Teams including my family helped mud out their house, removing sheetrock and ruined possessions. Ultimately, a church member who "flips houses" bought their home of forty-three years to make things a bit easier.

Brother John, as we affectionately called him, moved to Tennessee with his son and died eleven months later. In times like this, your identity *has* to be secure in Jesus or you'll never make it. Sure, you may replace the carpet and move back in, but you won't make it in the soul like Jesus wants.

At Brother John's memorial service, I quoted him saying, "I've preached it as long as I've been preaching, that 'Jesus is enough.' Now I've experienced it for myself. I've lost everything and it IS true: Jesus is still enough!" Wow! That's being anchored to a firm foundation. That's why he was such a difference maker.

Do you have an anchor?

Do you know how to use it?

The Bisagnos did; it was their identity in Jesus. Now reunited in heaven, they enjoy it even more.

Difference makers are secure in their identity, an identity that cannot be lost even in suffering. Can you imagine what the world would be like if Christians really and truly believed that we are eternally secure and on our way to eternal life? We wouldn't be afraid of death. We would risk everything for the sake of the gospel. We wouldn't gain the whole world and lose our souls; we would be willing to lose everything for the sake of Christ.

Can you imagine what the world would be like if Christians really believed that we are justified by faith? We wouldn't have to keep trying to justify ourselves. We wouldn't feel the need to win arguments. We would let go of offenses and let things roll off our backs. We wouldn't fight with the weapons of the world, but we would respond to offenses with grace and love.

Can you imagine if we really believed we were sons and daughters of God almighty, and that was the most fundamental thing about our identity? We would stop running to work or family or pleasure or entertainment to give us identity because we would already be completely secure in our identity. Then, we would actually be able to enjoy things like friends and family and work without putting on them the impossible expectation of fulfillment—an expectation they are far too fragile to bear.

Difference makers are secure in their identity. Through the floods and feasts they realize that what God says is true about them—loved, forgiven, adopted, justified—is not only true, but is the most fundamentally true thing about them. Thus, they are freed to go and make a difference in the world.

Never Alone

There is something else beautiful that comes with being God's people, the sheep of his pasture. It inherently means we are never alone. We are always in the company of both God and his people.

What more comforting picture could the Bible paint of God than that of a shepherd? As the true shepherd, Jesus not only comforts us, protects us, and provides for us, but he laid his life down for us. And as our shepherd, he is always with us.

This is the ministry of the Holy Spirit in our lives. Jesus told his disciples near the end of his time with them, "I will ask the Father, and he will give you another Counselor to be with you forever. He is the Spirit of truth" (John 14:16–17). This translation uses the word *Counselor*. Others might say *Comforter* or *Advocate*. The point is this: the Holy Spirit, when we become Christians, takes up residence among us and in us. He resides within us, comforting us, advocating for us, reminding us of the truth of the gospel. Because of his ministry and his presence, difference makers are never alone.

Not only do we have the presence of the Holy Spirit to comfort us, but we have one another. One of the mistakes I see so many Christians making today is trying to live the Christian life alone. But we were not made to do this. Hebrews 10:24–25 says, "Let us watch out for one another to provoke love and good works, not neglecting to gather together, as some are in the habit of doing, but encouraging each other, and all the more as you see the day approaching." This isn't only a clear command in the Bible—it's an assumption. The authors of the New Testament simply assumed that all Christians would be actively engaged in a local church, because when we become Christians, we become a part of a family. We are meant to live in community with brothers and sisters who will encourage us, challenge us, strengthen us, hold us accountable, mourn with us, celebrate with us, and remind us of the gospel we're all so prone to forget.

This takes the pressure off of us as difference makers. Making a difference seems like an impossible task on our own. Wouldn't it be daunting to think you had to do it all alone? But you don't. Difference makers know who they are. They are secure in their identity in Christ, and they know that, as his sheep, they are never alone.

Difference Makers Aren't Ashamed

Now, I want you to go back for a second to imagining you're an exiled Israelite. It would be pretty easy to be ashamed of who you are. If your identity were all about prospering in the Promised Land and now you're decaying in captivity, wouldn't you be embarrassed? Wouldn't you be ashamed? But that's not what we see in Psalm 79. The second part of verse 13 says, "We . . . will thank you forever; we will declare your praise to generation after generation."

They are not embarrassed here about being God's people. They're not hiding it. They're not saying, "Well, I'm like, kind of God's person, but it's a little embarrassing, so I'm not that excited about it." No, they proudly gave thanks to God and declared they were the people of God, the sheep of his pasture—even in such a difficult time.

Do you have an anchor?

Do you know how to use it?

There's two ditches we can fall into here if we're not careful. On the one hand, we could try to hide or minimize about being God's people in order to save social status. During the exile, God's people were taking a lot of losses, and as you look around at our culture, it may seem like we're taking a lot of losses. Our country continues to separate itself further and further from the Christian values upon which it was founded; there is less respect in the public square and in our educational institutions for a Christian worldview. Even in the churches, we've been devastated to see many revered Christian leaders fall amid public moral failure.

But we must remember, even as it seems we are losing all these battles, that God has already won the war. He won it at the cross.

A common phrase you hear in our culture is "the right side of history." You want to be "on the right side of history." Here's some good news for you, Christian: if you have faith in Jesus Christ, you are on the right side of history. At the end of the day, he will return and set right all that has been made wrong. He will bring justice to the world. He will defeat sin and Satan and death. And all those who have faith in him will live with him forever. This is good news. This means that we, as Christians, have nothing to be ashamed of; we can be proud to be the sheep of God's pasture. We can "declare your praise to generation after generation" without embarrassment, because no matter how bad it may seem now, he has already won the war.

However there is another ditch we may fall into. While we ought to be proud that we are God's people, we are not proud of ourselves, but of God. We must not have an arrogant or triumphalist attitude as though we are

God's people because we are better than everyone else. We must remember that we are "saved by grace through faith, and this is not from [ourselves]; it is God's gift—not from works, so that no one can boast" (Eph. 2:8–9). We were "dead in [our] trespasses and sins in which [we] previously lived according to the ways of this world" (Eph. 2:1–2). Paul says in Romans 3:23, "all have sinned and fall short of the glory of God." That levels the playing field. "All" includes you and me! He says in 1 Corinthians 6:

> Don't you know that the unrighteous will not inherit God's kingdom? Do not be deceived: No sexually immoral people, idolaters, adulterers, or males who have sex with males, no thieves, greedy people, drunkards, verbally abusive people, or swindlers will inherit God's kingdom. And some of you used to be like this. But you were washed, you were sanctified, you were justified in the name of the Lord Jesus Christ and by the Spirit of our God. (vv. 9–11)

Difference makers remember that they are no better than anyone else. The only difference in God's people and everyone else is that we were "washed . . . sanctified . . . justified . . . by the Spirit of our God." In other words, it's nothing we did. God did it. His Spirit gave us new hearts and brought us to life, so we have nothing to boast about. So we must not only avoid the ditch of being embarrassed about being God's people; we must also avoid the ditch of being prideful, as though we were better than everyone else. It's a fine line we walk as difference makers—a sort of humble boasting. Humble because we're saved by faith, but boasting, not in ourselves, but in the Lord.

Lost Sheep?

The disposition of a difference maker can be boiled down to this: we know we are not lost sheep. That's what it comes down to for people in this world. We have to answer the question: *Do we have a Shepherd, or are we all just lost sheep?* Difference makers know we have a Shepherd.

This changes how we see ourselves. It gives us a new disposition. It means we have a new identity as God's people. It means we're never alone. And it means we're not ashamed.

If you place your hope in your job or your spouse or your education or your physical body, what happens when you get fired, your spouse dies, or you lose your mental or physical faculties? You lose your identity. But in Jesus, we have an identity that no amount of suffering can take away from us. And not only that, but we have an identity that gives us a community—the Holy Spirit and the church. Difference makers don't have to feel the pressure to change the world on their own; we have the Holy Spirit and the church always present, always helping us. And in all of this, we can be proud, not of ourselves, but of the God who has called us to be his sheep.

CHAPTER 6

Purpose in Your Palace

Humanity is on a perpetual quest to discover our purpose. We all have this innate feeling that we were made for *something*, that we're supposed to do *something* important. But what?

This is one of the great struggles of modern society. Many people in our country believe the world came from nothing and will return to nothing, that human beings are just like any other animals, that we're random clumps of atoms with no soul and nothing to follow this life. Yet these same believers in a secular worldview have a feeling, the same God-given feeling that resonates with all of us—that they have a purpose. Or, as we put it in our Difference Maker Declaration, that we were all made for more than watching.

As Christians, we know we have a purpose. God created us, so he, as Creator, gets to define our purpose—lifting a heavy burden from us. We don't have to fret or worry or stress trying to discover or create a purpose; we can just look in God's Word and follow his voice as it leads.

I believe all Christians have two purposes: a general purpose and a personal purpose. Our general purpose is the same: to glorify God and to enjoy a relationship with him. That's why he created all of us, and he wants us to live into that purpose by loving him with all our heart, soul, strength, and mind (Deut. 6:5; Mark 12:30).

But I also believe each of us has a personal purpose. When we look at the great difference makers of history, we see people with a specific purpose: Abraham, Moses, David, Daniel, Mary, Paul—all of these people had amazing personal purposes in the plan of God.

So how can you discover your personal purpose? Let me propose a simple math equation:

$$\text{Character} + \text{Skill} + \text{Setting} = \text{Purpose}$$

The first component is your character. Are you increasing in godliness? Are you becoming more Christlike? Are you putting off the old person of sin and selfishness and increasingly pursuing holiness and service to God and others? That's a must. If you are going to live into your personal purpose, you must be a person of character and integrity. A wise church member of ours who is now in heaven used to say, "If you work on your testimony, God will work on your ministry." When you follow him deeply and consistently through the highs and lows, God is going to use you.

The second component is your skill set. We know that all of our skills are from God. He gives us natural gifts and abilities. He sovereignly puts us in families and schools and jobs and activities that increase and maximize certain skill sets. And he also gives us spiritual gifts for the edification of the church, as Paul says in 1 Corinthians 12:4–7. Regardless of how skilled or talented you feel, each of us has a particular skill set that contributes to our purpose.

Don't be too hard on yourself here. We all have something to contribute. You don't have to be the best to make an impact or have the joy of contributing; just getting in the game in faith is what he is looking for. I'm not the best counselor, but I still try to listen and help. I much prefer to talk than listen, but God can still use me to console and encourage. I'm not the greatest author in the world, but I'm writing with the hope God will use this book in your life. We are sometimes so driven to win that we fail to even try. God has equipped you and wants to use you. The fact that you aren't perfect or the best is to your spiritual advantage. God loves bad odds and weak vessels. Discover your gifts and put them to use.[1]

The final component of our purpose is our setting. Somebody who lived in Boston in the 1820s would not have the same personal purpose as someone in Tokyo in 2020 or Rome in 310. If you live in a rural area, your purpose may look different than if you live in a metropolitan area. If you are a wife and mother, your purpose will look different than a single person. None of these are better or more noble than others, but they are each unique, and each of them contributes to your personal purpose.

Our math problem could be refined to:

Godly Character + Your Gifts & Skills +
Your World = Eternal Purpose

Difference makers recognize and learn they have a purpose, and they live it. One of the most amazing stories of a difference maker in the Bible comes from an unlikely hero—a woman who realized her personal purpose.

For Such a Time as This

In Esther 4, we read a dramatic conversation between Queen Esther and her cousin Mordecai. Mordecai told Esther about an evil plot that would wipe out all of the Jewish people, and he begged Esther, as the queen, to go to the king and do something about it. In verse 13, we pick up with Mordecai's famous response:

> "Don't think that you will escape the fate of all the Jews because you are in the king's palace. If you keep silent at this time, relief and deliverance will come to the Jewish people from another place, but you and your father's family will be destroyed. *Who knows, perhaps you have come to your royal position for such a time as this.*" (vv. 13–14, emphasis added)

Esther had to decide whether to sit on the sidelines or be a difference maker. But how did we get here?

In the last chapter, we talked about the Babylonian exile. We said that in the year 586 BC, God's people were taken captive from their land and deported to Babylon. Not long after that, there was a changing of the guard at the top of the world superpower structure—the Babylonian Empire was replaced by the Persian Empire. The Israelites were still in exile, but now they were held captive by the Persians rather than the Babylonians.

The king of Persia was named Ahasuerus. He was a powerful king who had experienced great success and was not used to being told "no." But one of his wives, Queen Vashti, finally stood up to him and told him "no."

The king threw a massive party after a military success, and after drinking a bit too much wine, he summoned his wife. "He wanted to show off her beauty to the people and the officials" (Esther 1:11). In other words, the king wanted to treat his wife like an object and parade her around in front of his friends. The queen, apparently, had had enough. She refused. Tough woman. The result? She was cast out of the palace and replaced.

Essentially, the king had an elaborate, months-long beauty contest to determine who the next queen would be, and in God's providence, he raised up a beautiful, wise, young Jewish girl named Esther. Even in exile, God was preparing to use and to save his people.

Esther had a cousin named Mordecai who was like a father to her, but he had an enemy. The Bible tells us that a man named Haman hated Mordecai. Haman is described as an Agagite. This is one of those little facts that we can easily overlook as we read Scripture, but it's a very significant part of the story. The Agagites had been enemies of God's people for generations, and a couple hundred years prior to this, God commanded King Saul to put an end to these wicked people. You can read the story in 1 Samuel 15, where the same people are called the Amalekites; their king was named Agag, which is where we get the word *Agagite*.

Saul's God-given command was to put an end to the Amalekites and to kill King Agag, but he disobeyed. He left a number of those wicked people still alive, and because of his failure to finish what God told him, they were still around in the days of Esther. One of them in particular—Haman—still had it out for the Jews. Because of his hatred for Mordecai, he developed a plot to wipe out the entire Jewish people.

Haman put the plan together and tricked the king into enacting it. This is where we pick up in chapter 4. God was active and working for the good of his people. He placed Esther in the palace and gave her great influence, access to the king, and the ability to effect positive change. But Haman, the enemy of God and God's people, was working hard to destroy the Israelites. When Mordecai found out about the plan, he came to Esther and begged her to get off the sideline, to get in the game, and to be a difference maker.

"Who knows," Mordecai said to Esther, "perhaps you have come to your royal position for such a time as this" (v. 14). Esther pondered these words from Mordecai. She had to consider what her personal purpose was. She had godly character. God used her skill set to land her in the palace. Now she had to consider her setting. Perhaps it was for this very purpose, Mordecai told her, that she had been placed in this setting—so that God might use her to save his people.

And that is exactly what happened. Esther got off the sideline. She got in the game. She resolved to be used by God. She approached the king, and God used her to save his people. We can learn much about being a difference maker from this story of Esther.

Strive for the Palace

Sometimes I think Christians are afraid of influence. But God wants difference makers in the palace. He wants to raise us up to places of influence so we can make a positive wallop on the world. Difference makers need godly ambition—to strive for a consequential place in the palace. Be the president, CEO, Hollywood star, or team mom!

> Every Christian must consciously commit to impacting the culture. To do that requires influence. Influence is not an automatic gift bestowed on good people. It is earned. It falls to a huge variety of people, most of whom consciously plan on acquiring influence. Christians need to seek influence. They need to acquire it. They need to use it once they have it.
> —Hugh Hewitt[2]

But understand the difference in godly ambition and selfish ambition. Selfish ambition is a lust and a desire to work really hard for yourself. At its core it is gross pride, not godly praise. Man, this can be tough. I've felt it. Is my desire to succeed for me or God? Often I have prayed, "Lord, I desire Christian faithfulness, not vocational success in this endeavor." If your personality craves accomplishment, this is even more troublesome.

Godliness is not a beckoning to run from accomplishment and influence. Win the award, close the deal, make a ton of money, grow the ministry . . . but do it for God's purposes, not to offset your insecurities. The internal *why* of the trophy tells us more about ourselves than the accomplishment. Some of the most successful men in the world are really little boys still looking for their dad's approval. You have your heavenly Father's approval, so live differently. As I often tell my kids, "You are living FROM your father's approval, not FOR your father's approval."

Esther's influence turns the palace on its head. She is not seeking to get her face on a coin as queen or Mordecai's approval but fearfully following God in his call to action. Godly ambition is eternal in the tremor it produces, while our selfish ambition is a tarnishing trophy. Literally, our ambition is fading while we are pursuing it.

In the same way, the rich man will wither away *while pursuing* his activities. (James 1:11, emphasis added)

To prevent this, let's define godly ambition. Godly ambition is a drive that seeks first the glory of God and second the good of others. It is a pursuit of excellence and influence, not for selfish or earthly gain, but in order to leverage that influence for the glory of God and the good of our fellow men and women. This is the kind of ambition that drives difference makers; this is what it means to strive for the palace.

Now, I want to speak clearly here: everybody's palace is different. Your palace might be making movies in Hollywood, reporting for a major media outlet, or teaching first graders how to read and write. Your palace might be in politics, in ministry, or in health care. Everybody's palace looks different because everybody's personal purpose is unique. The pursuit of the palace, then, is not a pursuit of a particular setting; it's about living into our personal purpose. It's an attitude that is determined to be excellent in all things and to leverage the influence God has given you—whatever that influence looks like. Your life's goal is not to live in a certain neighborhood (setting) but love your neighbors (purpose).

Don't be afraid of that influence! Don't be content to sit on the sidelines and root for other people as they make a difference. Be ambitious in the right way; strive for the top because you desire godly influence, not personal gain. This is exactly what Mordecai told Esther. "If you keep silent at this time, relief and deliverance will come to the Jewish people from another place" (Esther 4:14). Mordecai knew God was powerful. He knew God would still accomplish his purposes and protect his people. But he wanted Esther to live into her purpose and be the vessel through whom God did his work.

Let me issue the same challenge to you. Don't be content to sit on the sidelines, watching God do his work through others. Jump in the river of God's sovereign work in the world. Be a part of his plans and purposes. We desperately need godly people living in DC shaping politics, in NYC impacting business, in LA shaping the entertainment culture, and, FYI, we need it on your street too. Be a difference maker in your palace, even if it is a cubicle, classroom, or condo.

Once You're in the Palace . . .

I said a moment ago that I think Christians are afraid of influence, and I encouraged you not to be so. But now I want to empathize. I understand why some people are afraid of influence. I've felt guilt at times for the blessings and settings I've been in. I have nice things and have been a part of amazing opportunities. My refrigerator is full while other children of God are looking for their next meal. Instead of being paralyzed by "why me" guilt, I need to realize the palace comes with unique opportunities and temptations.

A funny thing often happens to us when God has placed us in the palace. We often shift from grateful impact to protective maintenance.

Our goal on the way to the palace is grateful impact. We want to make a difference. We want to share the gospel of Jesus. We want to improve the lives of others. We want to glorify God and make much of him. But once we've been in the palace a while, we start to get comfortable. And we shift to a mind-set of protective maintenance.

We start building moats.

When we start building moats, we know we've lost sight of God's purpose for us. We are no longer leveraging our character, skills, and setting for his glory, but for ours. Trying to mask or mend the hurts we've coddled and despised for years, we seek a comfortable castle. When we build moats, we ignore God's calling and we keep other people out or maybe better said, we keep ourselves in . . . our bubble. We avoid anything that makes us uncomfortable, anything that stretches, and anyone who does not contribute something positive or useful to the vision that we've created for our lives.

Jesus tells a parable in Luke 16 about a man who got too comfortable in the palace. We know the parable as the story of the rich man and Lazarus.

The rich man had been blessed by God with great wealth and possessions—he was living in the palace. But he used the palace for his own enjoyment, not for the mission of God. So every day when he passed by the sick, impoverished beggar Lazarus—someone the rich man thought couldn't add anything useful to his life—the rich man ignored him and trotted back up to his palace.

Truthfully, the rich man is easily us. The fact you are reading and have more than twenty dollars to your name in worldwide standards means you are rich. My kids asked me a while back, "Dad, are we rich?" to which I answered, "Yep." Not by Silicon Valley's standards, but in comparison to the world, yep. The theme of living in the palace is not guilt, but leveraged impact. For example, I can and do sponsor a child's education in India and two in Africa with the vision of reversing their statistical story by the power of Jesus using me.[3]

Of course, this is a story of great reversal just as Esther is; in the next life, we see Lazarus in heaven being comforted and the rich man in agony. The rich man, we are told, received his good things on earth. Because he was so self-focused, worried about maintaining and pre-serving his palace, he was blind to the glory of God and the needs of other people.

An interesting note about this parable is that we're told the beggar's name—Lazarus. But we don't know the rich man's name. And this is what happens when we shift to protective maintenance: we become a category. We lose our unique and personal calling, and we become a category: "The rich man."

Friends, don't become a category. Don't be content with sitting on the sidelines like the rich man who refused to be a difference maker. Instead, be a person with a name and a purpose like Esther.

Esther decided not to worry about preserving her position in the palace; she decided instead to leverage her position in the palace. That is what difference makers do.

After listening to the wisdom and advice of her cousin Mordecai, Esther came to an amazing place. She came to a place of being willing to risk her place in the palace. She determined to approach the king and save her people. And her words to Mordecai were amazing: "If I perish, I perish" (Esther 4:16).

Esther took an inventory of her character, her skills, and her setting. She recognized a great need. She recognized that God was inviting her, not to sit on the sidelines, but to be a difference maker, so she jumped in the game. And God did the rest.

Risk It All

Are you willing to risk it all like Esther? Are you willing to strive for the palace and, once you're there, not protectively maintain your position, but leverage it for the glory of God and the good of others?

When Esther committed to this plan, she did not know what was going to happen. She didn't know if the king would receive her uninvited presence or sentence her to the death penalty for it. Even if he did accept her, she didn't know if her people would be saved. And you and I don't know the future either. Are you willing to say, "If I perish, I perish"?

You may be in the palace right now with your job, your financial situation, your education, your family—and a risk may cost you everything. What if you risk it all? What if you lose it all? The history of the church is full of martyrs who, like Esther, said, "If I perish, I perish." But unlike Esther, they actually did perish. But this was not a mistake. The reality of life with Jesus is, it would be better to get in the game and lose our lives than to stay on the sidelines. Remember the words of Jesus: "Whoever would save his life will lose it, but whoever loses his life for my sake will find it" (Matt. 16:25 ESV).

When I graduated from Texas A&M, I was unsure of what I would do, as many students are. Everyone else seemed to have secured jobs in their appropriate fields. But I felt that I was to stay to continue leading a college Bible study that my roommates and I started our sophomore year. It was a risk-it-all decision in my life to forgo looking for a "real job" and stick with our growing ministry. As paychecks rolled in for my friends, as they too followed the Lord's direction on their path, donations to this upstart trickled in for me. To make ends meet, I began to substitute teach during the day in order to minister to students at night. Every once in a while I would lead a church retreat and make a few hundred dollars and gas money. My W-2 form that year showed a whopping $7,000. But fulfilling your purpose is better than money.

The ministry was bearing fruit, as the tens had turned into hundreds of students each week in this ministry we called Breakaway. More than a decade later, I was directing a ministry to thousands each week, traveling the country speaking, and married with a son to raise. The risk-it-all moment was blossoming into a palace to keep leveraging.

Fast-forward twenty-nine years to the week I'm typing this, and Breakaway is stronger than ever. I stood with my wife and now two kids in the Texas A&M basketball stadium as eight thousand college students flooded in—the faithfulness of God on display. Just like Esther, if I hadn't risked it all, God would have used someone else. But he didn't! He used me. I had a front-row seat to the most incredible journey. Not just a journey of ministry growth, but a joy-fulfilling journey of his purpose in my life. Incredible!

Esther took a risk and in God's sovereignty it paid off. That's what difference makers do. God has plans of impact for you too. Risk it. Follow him all the way. You never know how he can use you. Leverage your palace for his plan. Quit hiding behind moats and experience what and Who you were made for.

CHAPTER 7

The Give-and-Go

One of the most common and time-tested plays in team sports is the give-and-go. It's fundamental in basketball in its beauty and simplicity. One player starts with the ball—passes it to another player, and immediately after passing, when the first player's defender might have his or her guard down, the first player makes a move and goes toward the goal. Pippen and Jordan, Bird and McHale, and Kobe and Shaq have bought mansions and Ferraris on this.

As common and effective as the give-and-go is in basketball, it's even more effective in the life of a difference maker. Unfortunately, it's much less common.

No, I'm not talking about a two-man play that leads to easy points, but there is a give-and-go to following Jesus. Every single one of us, as his follower, is called to give and to go. We see this in the life of Jesus, who set the ultimate example for us.

The Give-and-Go of Jesus

How did Jesus give? Remember in the last chapter when we saw Esther risk her place in the palace for the sake of her people? Jesus didn't simply risk his place in the palace; he gave up his place in the heavenly palace. He gave up the privileges that came with being God and emptied himself, taking on a human form and giving his very life. Jesus didn't just give a little bit; he gave all.

So he is our example. The give-and-go of a Christ follower is about giving up ourselves for the glory of God and the good of others, and it's about going wherever God has called us to go.

Jesus gave and went on our behalf. From eternity past, Jesus was in heaven with God the Father and God the Holy Spirit. He had everything he could ever want or need. But he left. He came to earth, was born of the Virgin Mary, and lived a human life. He did not cease to be God, but he added a human nature to himself, so that he is the only person ever to have two natures—a divine nature and a human nature. But he didn't stop with coming from heaven to earth; the reason Jesus came to earth was to go somewhere specific. He came to go to the cross.

At the cross, Jesus accepted the punishment that we deserved for our sins, so that we might be forgiven. He traded places with us. He bore our punishment and the wrath of God so that we, if we believe in him, can not only avoid the punishment we deserve, but can receive the reward that he deserves as the perfect, obedient Son of God.

The reality is, we're all giving and going somewhere. Get on the interstate on a Monday morning or go to the mall on a Saturday afternoon. Everyone is going and giving their time and resources, and you're no exception. It's a matter of choosing where we will go and to what we will give. And we see a great example of this in another difference-maker story in the Old Testament—the story of Ezra.

Ezra

In the last two chapters, we've talked about the exile of God's people, how they were removed from the Promised Land because of their disobedience and idolatry and taken to a different land. In chapter 5, we learned that difference makers maintain a certain disposition even when things are hard, even in exile. In chapter 6, we saw how God raised up Esther in exile and placed her in the palace, and how he called her to risk it all from the palace for his glory and the good of others. In this chapter we see the beginning of the end of exile—how God worked to bring his people back to the Promised Land.

You can read this whole amazing story in the Old Testament books of Ezra and Nehemiah. Both of these men—Ezra and Nehemiah—were difference makers who left a beautiful legacy of obedience to God. But in this chapter, I'm not going to focus too much on either of them personally; I'm going to focus on the difference-making legacy of the people of Israel as God returned them from exile.

In chapter 1 of Ezra, we read that God stirred the heart of King Cyrus of Persia to release the Israelites from captivity. This is an amazing thing about God—he has power even over people who don't recognize him as Lord. Cyrus was not a believer in the one true God; he worshiped false gods and idols. But God nonetheless "roused the spirit of King Cyrus to issue a proclamation throughout his entire kingdom" (Ezra 1:1). This is a living example of the truth we read in Proverbs 21:1: "A king's heart is like channeled water in the LORD's hand: He directs it wherever he chooses." God has complete control over the heart, the emotions, the decisions, and the actions of even those people who reject him and worship other gods.

So what did this proclamation of King Cyrus say?

> This is what King Cyrus of Persia says:
> "The LORD, the God of the heavens, has
> given me all the kingdoms of the earth

and has appointed me to build him a house at Jerusalem in Judah. Any of his people among you, may his God be with him, and may he go to Jerusalem in Judah and build the house of the LORD, the God of Israel, the God who is in Jerusalem. Let every survivor, wherever he resides, be assisted by the men of that region with silver, gold, goods, and livestock, along with a freewill offering for the house of God in Jerusalem." (Ezra 1:2–4)

Are you kidding me? Not only is Cyrus letting God's people return to their land, he's paying for them to rebuild the temple! And here's how God would do this: not just by the power of one person, but by the collective power of thousands of difference makers who decided to give and go. Verses 5–6 tells us:

So the family heads of Judah and Benjamin, along with the priests and Levites—everyone whose spirit God had roused—prepared to go up and rebuild the LORD's house in Jerusalem. All their neighbors *supported* [*gave*] them with silver articles, gold, goods, livestock, and valuables, in addition to all that was given as a freewill offering. (emphasis added)

I hope you saw it in those two verses. The first group was the goers. They were called by God to go back to Jerusalem and work to rebuild the temple. The second group was the givers. They funded the trip and the building project. Friends, we see here a crystal-clear picture of the give-and-go of Jesus. And as the Israelites marched back to the Promised Land to take on the task of rebuilding the temple, I like to imagine them saying together:

> *I was made for more than watching. I have a history-changing, difference-making, life-giving, Spirit-empowered legacy to leave. Jesus, I ask you to work deeply in me and clearly through me as I pray, give, and go in your love. I am a difference maker. In Jesus' name. Amen.*

Give

Christians are not all called to give equally, but we are called to give.

We see this in verse six of Ezra 1. While some were returning to the Promised Land, all the neighbors supplied them "with silver articles, gold, goods, livestock, and valuables, in addition to all that was given as a freewill offering."

There is a clear biblical calling for all followers of Jesus to give generously. This expectation is not limited to our money. We are expected to be generous with our time, our possessions, our abilities—with everything. As Paul puts it in Romans 12, "In view of the mercies of God, I urge you to present your bodies as a living sacrifice, holy and pleasing to God; this is your true worship" (v. 1). True worship is defined by Paul here as giving *everything*—our whole selves—to God for him to use as he pleases.

We can only come to this place of generosity by realizing that nothing is ours to begin with. "Every animal of the forest is mine, the cattle on a thousand hills" (Ps. 50:10). What is God saying? That he has a farm with a thousand hills and he owns all that cattle? Of course not. This is a figure of speech, a way of saying that God owns all the cattle on all the hills. The sheep too. That's us. *Baaa!*

And if he owns all the cattle on all the hills, he owns all of the money in our bank accounts, all the time on our calendars, all the clothes in our closets, food in our pantries, cars in our garages, and literally everything else.

What does this mean for us? It means that we're simply stewards or managers of God's possessions. And stewards, as Paul reminds his readers in 1 Corinthians 4, must "be found faithful" (v. 2).

As faithful stewards of God's possessions, our hearts need to be where his heart is. We need to spend on the things he would spend on, to give toward the causes he is involved in, to share with the people as he would share with them.

Jim Elliot famously wrote, "He is no fool who gives that which he cannot keep to gain that which he cannot lose."[1] If we don't own anything and are simply stewards of God's possessions, then we aren't going to keep anything—all that we have will be required of us when we stand before God, and we will have to give an account for it. Difference makers know this, and it leads them to a life of generosity.

Now you may be thinking to yourself, *This guy doesn't know my situation. He doesn't know how much debt I have, how little I have to scrape by on, or the fact that I'm raising three kids as a single parent. How could I ever live a generous life?* I want to encourage you in two ways.

First, know that generosity starts with the heart. In Mark 12, we read a story that is no doubt familiar to many of us:

> Sitting across from the temple treasury, [Jesus] watched how the crowd dropped money into the treasury. Many rich people were putting in large sums. Then a poor widow came and dropped in two tiny

coins worth very little. Summoning his disciples, he said to them, "Truly I tell you, this poor widow has put more into the treasury than all the others. For they all gave out of their surplus, but she out of her poverty has put in everything she had—all that she had to live on." (vv. 41–44)

Translated into today's money, this woman gave the equivalent of about three dollars. Most of us would consider that a measly gift. But it was all she had, and because of her generous heart, she desired to give it to God. Jesus recognized this, and he said that her gift was worth more than all those who gave out of their prosperity.

Remember, God owns everything, so he doesn't want the big flashy gifts for others' eyes. The million-dollar gift is less impressive to God than the two-coin gift when it is for men's eyes not God's heart. What God is most interested in is a generous heart, and you can have that even if you don't have much in your bank account.

Second, I want you to know that it's never too late to start living generously. Start by giving a certain percentage of your income each month. It may not be much by the suburban American standards, but if it comes from a generous heart, it is pleasing to God. And every six months step up a percentage point and watch God open the heavens for you.

If you are in a tough financial situation, get help. Ask your pastor to connect you with someone in your church who can teach you how to budget, how to work your way out of debt and toward giving more. It will be hard and it will require sacrifice, but it is worth it, because we were made to live generously.

The flip side of the coin is, many of us have plenty of money but are either holding it or wasting it. We spend more on our cell phone and cable TV package than we give to our church.

Art Rainer, author of several books about faith and finances, says, "God designed us to be generous. And He designed us to be generous in ways that expand His Kingdom. God designed us not to be hoarders but to be conduits through which His generosity flows."[2] What's standing between you and a life of generosity?

Go

Not long ago, the Southeastern Baptist Theological Seminary in Wake Forest, North Carolina, created a new slogan: *I Am Going.* The mission behind this motto is this:

> We seek to glorify the Lord Jesus Christ
> by equipping students to serve the Church
> and fulfill the Great Commission.[3]

I love this motto and mission, because they are right in line with what we are all called to as Christians. The aim of God's work in the world right now is seen in the Great Commission: "*Go*, therefore, and make disciples of all nations, baptizing them in the name of the Father and of the Son and of the Holy Spirit, teaching them to observe everything I have commanded you" (Matt. 28:19–20, emphasis added). If this is God's goal, then it is our goal too.

This is the aim of a difference maker's life. A difference maker realizes that life isn't the sum of all her experiences or possessions. It isn't about fame or friends or followers on social media. The aim of life is the Great Commission. The call of life is to go.

We must realize that all of us are called to go *somewhere*. I'm not saying to sell your house. Your address may remain, but we are still on the go of the gospel. Where you are called to go is dependent on your personal purpose. Remember our equation from the last chapter: Character + Skills + Setting = Purpose. All of us are called to go, and your purpose reveals where you specifically are called to go.

Some difference makers are called to vocational ministry. Notice in Ezra 1:5 that not everybody returned right away, but only those "whose spirit God had roused." Have you ever felt a rousing in your spirit like that? Do you have a nagging feeling that you're supposed to be preaching or planting churches, serving in kids' ministry or as a missionary? The nineteenth-century English pastor and preacher Charles Spurgeon said the first sign of a call to ministry is "an intense, all-absorbing desire for the work." Do you have that desire? Is that where your mind goes when you're dreaming? If so, let me encourage you from someone who's been doing it for more than thirty years: *it's amazing!* Don't get me wrong, it can be demanding. It's a challenging, anxiety-inducing, and at times, a heavy calling. But it's also thrilling, encouraging, and the most gratifying thing you can imagine. If God is calling you to ministry as a job, there's no better place you could be.

But not everyone will go into vocational ministry. In fact, the vast majority of Christians won't. BUT all Christians are called to the ministry—it's just through a thousand different job descriptions. We've too deeply separated the clergy from the pews as if one is holy and the other is common.

A prominent NCAA commercial a few years back included the following tagline: "There are more than 400,000 NCAA student-athletes, and most of us will go pro in something other than sports."[4] There are literally billions of Christians in the world, and most of us "go pro" in something other than preaching. You may be called to be a lawyer, a teacher, a janitor, a chef, or an electrician—the list is truly endless. But you are in the ministry because you love Jesus.

Regardless of where you are called to go, we all have the same overarching goal. Just as we all have the same general purpose but unique personal purposes, we all have the same goal as we go—the Great Commission.

So how should you see your work in light of that call to go? How should you see your parenting, your school work, or your relationship with your neighbors, friends, or family in light of the call to go? Remember, whatever your personal purpose is, model your life after Jesus, the ultimate example of what it means to go.

A Challenge

Some of you may be wondering, *If God really doesn't need anything from me, why is he asking me to give and go so much? Why doesn't he just do it on his own?* Here's the answer: God doesn't need anything *from* you; he wants something *for* you. We were not made to be satisfied with the little trinkets this life has to offer. Hoarding temporary worldly treasures of money and comfort will not satisfy our souls. The great twentieth-century author C. S. Lewis said:

> It would seem that Our Lord finds our desires not too strong, but too weak. We

are half-hearted creatures, fooling about with drink and sex and ambition when infinite joy is offered us, like an ignorant child who wants to go on making mud pies in a slum because he cannot imagine what is meant by the offer of a holiday at the sea. We are far too easily pleased.[5]

Friend, if you are refusing to give and go because you think doing so will cause you to miss out, please hear this: your refusal to give and go is causing you to miss out on what really matters. You are like a child playing in mud in the slums when God has invited you to a holiday at the sea—the adventure of a lifetime. Don't miss out on your purpose. Don't get stuck hoarding what God has given you. Be a difference maker.

Pastor and author John Piper says there are only three kinds of Christians: "zealous goers, zealous senders, and disobedient."[6] In light of this convicting truth, let me close this chapter with a challenge related to going and a challenge related to giving.

Let me challenge you to reconsider where God is calling you to go. Reconsider your purpose. It's possible that God has you exactly where you're called. Maybe being a stay-at-home mom, an accountant, or a math teacher is precisely where he wants you. But maybe he is calling you to something different. Maybe he is calling your family to move to the other side of town and do life and ministry with people different than yourself. Maybe he's calling you to the other side of the world, to plant a church in an atheist country or a Muslim country or a Hindu country. Maybe he's calling you to the pastorate. Would you carefully, prayerfully, and in discussion with your church community, consider again where God is calling you? And will you commit to being obedient to whatever you hear? It is not about changing our address but changing our perspective. God wants to make a difference through you in a gated neighborhood or one with gangs. He's placed you for a purpose (Acts 17:26–27).

Let me also challenge you in relation to your giving. Think about it like this: What is the biggest expense you have each month? Most likely, it is where you live or what you drive. What if you set a goal of your generosity rivaling that expenditure? Your biggest outflow to become giving to the Lord's work. It would take some work, but what fun it would be! This may sound absurd to you right now, but I bet you can get there over time. Start small, save, work, and ask God for courage.

Whether generosity is your biggest outflow each month or not, be a faithful giver. Not only with your financial resources but your encouraging words, helpful hands, listening ears, and precious time.

Let me give you an example of difference makers in these realms from an unexpected angle. Our church has an incredible special needs ministry. Several years ago we couldn't figure out how best to serve these families. Nothing seemed to fit until we decided to go for it and take a step of faith to hire a director and dedicate space in our building to our "Through the Roof" ministry. The name is based on the account of the paralyzed man being lowered "though the roof" in Luke 5:19. The man needed the help of his friends so they showed ingenuity and hard work to get him to Jesus. Our kids (and adults) with special needs require friends at church to help them too.

With the ministry up and running we began a "buddy" program to connect our older elementary through high school kids to our special needs kids to be their buddy on Sundays. Incredible discipleship for both to connect these groups. So now "Through the Roof" is not that "kinda different and scary unknown ministry down the hall" but a place of friendship.

Now that you have the context, let's see the book of Ezra come alive today. I can remember the moment in my office looking at the build-out plans for the space. It included a custom playground, special rooms and toys . . . the works. Of course, it cost more than we planned and took more space than we thought. But I remember my sentence, "We can't do enough for these families. Let's do it!" It was as if Gabriel then declared to angels, "They took a step of faith; go get the difference makers to make it happen."

The money was miraculously given through church members' generosity and particularly a family who doesn't even have a special needs kid. They, more important, had a heart for impact and sharing! And now families in challenging situations are ministered to each week. Also, our buddy program is a highlight of serving others. Our students have become difference makers as they give one-on-one care to teach their special friends. Instead of making fun, they are making friends.

It blessed me to hear of one little girl telling her parents stories of her "buddy" and all they did that day on the drive home from church. There is excitement in her voice as she is learning to give and go. Her parents are encouraged as well. As her heart has grown she has decided to give 50 percent of her allowance to the Lord's work. It is giving and going at its best. What a joy to watch! We can learn so much from the heart of children. Let's take a step of giving and going in our lives too. Let's be like the people of Ezra.

As we've seen in the opening verses of the book of Ezra and with this little girl, being a difference maker isn't reserved for elite Christians, or people with amazing and unique talents. The call to be a difference maker is given to all of us. It's a call to follow the example of our Savior: to give and go. You will find no greater joy, challenge, or fulfillment!

CHAPTER 8

Running to Trouble

Every few years there seems to be a new scare of some outbreak that is bound to end the world. There was bird flu. Then there was swine flu. Or maybe swine flu was first—it's hard to keep track. In 2016 there was a notable outbreak of the Zika virus, which kept many fans and some athletes away from the summer Olympics. And in 2014, there was the Ebola outbreak in Africa.

None of these outbreaks have had quite the apocalyptic affect on society that many predicted, but they were nonetheless serious at the time. Tragically, the Ebola outbreak in West Africa, which lasted until 2016, ended with 28,600 confirmed cases and 11,325 deaths.[1]

An interesting thing happened in the summer of 2014 when the Ebola outbreak was at its peak. As countless travelers returned home and precautionary measures stretched to the extreme, certain groups of Christians kept going. The *Christian Examiner* reported on October 3 of that year, "Many church groups and denominational ministries are resolved to continue ongoing work in the affected areas."[2] The United Methodist Church committed to distribute "love, food, and information" to those affected by the outbreak. The Lutheran Church Missouri Synod stepped up to partner with the Evangelical Lutheran Church in Sierra Leone to provide relief and meet needs. The Assemblies of God denomination and Southern Baptists took a similar approach.

While the whole world was running from trouble, Christians were running to it.

I saw this firsthand in Houston during the aftermath of Hurricane Harvey. Don't get me wrong, we got lots of help from people of all kinds of different cultural and religious backgrounds, but Jesus-loving, Spirit-empowered, difference-making Christians went above and beyond.

In an article titled "How Southern Baptists Trained More Disaster Relief Volunteers than the Red Cross," Sarah Eekhoff Zylstra reported that "the Southern Baptist Convention's disaster response is so massive it financially trails only the Red Cross and Salvation Army—and has more trained disaster relief volunteers than either one."[3] Those in Houston affected by the storm certainly felt that massive force as it descended upon our city with loving hearts and open hands, ready to help in any and every way possible. *USA Today* reported 80 percent of the assistance in Harvey was from nonprofit groups and most of them faith-based.[4] Just our church has hosted more than one hundred mission teams from around the country to serve flood victims.

So it seems that Christians have a funny way of running to trouble. This is a mark of a difference maker. We already saw that Jesus came not to heal those who are well, but those who are sick; not to save the righteous, but sinners. That's why he came, and that's why we go. Likewise, people who aren't experiencing any trouble—people who have it all together physically, emotionally, financially—don't need a ton of help. So difference makers have their eyes open for trouble, and instead of running away from it, retreating to safety, they run to it. We are running to help both physically and, most important, spiritually.

Lukewarm Christians

Do you remember the first line of the Difference Maker Declaration? Let's look back at it and refresh our memory:

> *I was made for more than watching. I have a history-changing, difference-making, life-giving, Spirit-empowered legacy to leave. Jesus, I ask you to work deeply in me and clearly through me as I pray, give, and go in*

your love. I am a difference maker. In Jesus'
name. Amen.

That first line is so important: *I was made for more
than watching.* I'm afraid that many of us, especially in the
United States, have bought into a version of Christianity
that lets us get by with just watching, with sitting on the
sidelines.

The American Dream is a vision of what the "good
life" looks like. It normally involves home ownership in
a safe neighborhood, 2.5 kids, a dog (but definitely no
cats!), and enough stocked away in a savings account to
retire by age sixty-five. As Americans, we believe that
anybody can achieve this if he or she works hard enough.
It becomes our goal, the main thing we're striving toward
in life. It is wonderful to live in a land of opportunity for
all, but we don't want to settle into forgetting we are first
people of the soul, not stuff.

If a material dream is the main thing we're striving
for, the words of Jesus sound increasingly foreign to us.
What do we do with the following sayings of Christ if the
American Dream is our highest goal?

- "It is easier for a camel to go through
  the eye of a needle than for a rich
  person to enter the kingdom of God"
  (Mark 10:25).

- "If anyone comes to me and does not hate his own father and mother, wife and children, brothers and sisters— yes, even his own life—he cannot be my disciple. Whoever does not bear his own cross and come after me cannot be my disciple" (Luke 14:26–27).
- "For whoever would save his life will lose it, but whoever loses his life for my sake will find it" (Matt. 16:25 ESV).

Whenever we try to combine biblical Christianity and the American Dream, we get a third result, something that doesn't quite look like either of the first two. We end up sanitizing the words of Jesus and feeling guilty for owning nice things—we memorize John 3:16, rejoicing that we have eternal life, but we don't take seriously the call of Jesus to follow him *now*. We end up practicing lukewarm Christianity that is a weird combination of guilt, greed, and desire to help others. This is what Jesus said to a lukewarm church in the book of Revelation:

"I know your works, that you are neither cold nor hot. I wish that you were cold or hot. So, because you are lukewarm, and neither hot nor cold, I am going to vomit you out of my mouth. For you say, 'I'm rich; I have become wealthy and need nothing,' and you don't realize that you are wretched, pitiful, poor, blind, and naked." (Rev. 3:15–17)

If our main goal in life is achieving the American Dream or some other worldly vision of flourishing, we will become so focused on gaining physical, temporal wealth that we will be spiritually "wretched, pitiful, poor, blind, and naked." In a chapter of his book *Crazy Love* called "Profile of the Lukewarm," Francis Chan says:

> Lukewarm people are thankful for their luxuries and comforts, and rarely consider trying to give as much as possible to the poor. They are quick to point out, "Jesus never said money is the root of all evil, only that the *love* of money is." Untold numbers of lukewarm people feel "called" to minister to the rich; very few feel "called" to minister to the poor.[5]

The bottom line is this: lukewarm Christians tend to run away from trouble when it surpasses their comfort level, rather than running to it. They retreat to their comforts, rather than sacrificing for those who need it. To be real difference makers, we have to push past convenience or feeling good into God-first sacrifice.

Looking for Trouble

Chris Rice has a great song, "Me and Becky," that illustrates the challenges we all feel of living for Jesus and living in the United States, including *me*. Becky, in the song, lives on "Abundant Life Boulevard." She has everything she needs from an earthly perspective. But she faces the temptation to leave behind a world "full of souls as important as yours and mine."

Now, before you go sell your house and all your possessions, hear me out. Having wealth and possessions isn't the problem. I have a filled closet and fridge, nice house and cars, investments and vacations planned. So don't hear me pointing fingers. In fact, the apostle Paul assumed that some Christians would. "Instruct those who are rich in the present age," he says in 1 Timothy, "not to be arrogant or to set their hope on the uncertainty of wealth, but on God, who richly provides us with all things to enjoy. Instruct them to do what is good, to be rich in good works, to be generous and willing to share, storing up treasure for themselves as a good foundation for the coming age, so that they may take hold of what is truly life" (6:17–19). The instruction for the wealthy, then is not necessarily to give everything away; it is to do good. Our heart's treasure is the issue. In other words, to put it in the context of the Difference Maker Declaration, we are called to get off the sideline. We are called to run to trouble.

But to run to trouble, we have to know where to find it. We have to look for it. We have to live with open eyes.

One of the great tragedies of the American Dream is that it creates an insulated life. We can go to church each Sunday, sit in the same row next to our same few friends, go to the same Sunday school class with the others who have been in it for a decade, and do the same thing week after week. We can get up and go to work or school each day, come home, open up the garage door, pull in, and head straight inside without ever having to interact with our neighbors. We can, essentially, close our eyes to the world around us and just do our own thing.

But that's not what difference makers are called to do. Difference makers are called to keep their eyes open, to look for trouble, internal or external, and to run to it.

Looking in the Word

How can you start to look for trouble? How can you get off the sidelines? The first place you should go is to God in prayer and in his Word. If you are getting a steady diet of God's Word every single day, God will reveal to you where to look for trouble and how to run to it.

Let me challenge you to increase your Bible intake. Maybe you've been inconsistent in reading the Bible; you want to read it every day, but you normally only do it two or three times a week. You get busy, you get distracted, you need to sleep in. Or maybe you're great about reading it every day, but you only read one or two verses that pop up on your Bible app as the "verse of the day." I don't want to discourage you or be too hard on you here, but if we really believe the sixty-six books of the Bible contain God's Word for us, won't we do more? Won't we push harder?

Here are a few tips:

- Try to read the Bible in a year or at least the New Testament.
- Read the Bible with someone. Meeting once a week or even talking on the phone once a week will give you accountability and spur you on to keep reading.
- Pick a time and pick a spot. Don't vary. If you are consistent in when and where you read the Bible, you're more likely to do it every day.
- Read a chapter in the morning and another at night.

Consistency creates a cumulative effect in your life. You won't be able to mark the day, but you will see the change. As you commit to reading the Bible and continue to do so, you will, over time, come across all kinds of commands from God about the kinds of people and situations you should be running to and serving.

- "You must not mistreat any widow or fatherless child" (Exod. 22:22).
- "Love the sojourner, therefore, for you were sojourners in the land of Egypt" (Deut. 10:19 ESV).
- God in his holy dwelling is a father of the fatherless and a champion of widows. God provides homes for those who are deserted. He leads out the prisoners to prosperity, but the rebellious live in a scorched land (Ps. 68:5–6).
- "Then the King will say to those on his right, 'Come, you who are blessed by my Father; inherit the kingdom prepared for you from the foundation of the world. For I was hungry and you gave me something to eat; I was thirsty and you gave me something to drink; I was a stranger and you took me in; I was naked and you clothed me; I was sick and you took care of me; I

was in prison and you visited me.' . . . Truly I tell you, whatever you did for one of the least of these brothers and sisters of mine, you did for me'" (Matt. 25:34–36, 40).

- Pure and undefiled religion before God the Father is this: to look after orphans and widows in their distress and to keep oneself unstained from the world (James 1:27).

- If anyone has this world's goods and sees a fellow believer in need but withholds compassion from him— how does God's love reside in him? Little children, let us not love in word or speech, but in action and in truth (1 John 3:17–18).

As you continually read and submit to God's Word for the rest of your life, ask him to show you where and how to be a difference maker. Ask him what it looks like for you to serve the widow and the orphan, the sojourners, the hungry, thirsty, naked, and imprisoned, the stranger, and fellow believers in need. As you ask him to make you a difference maker and to point you to where you can make a difference, he will be faithful.

Looking in the World

In addition to looking for trouble in the Word, we can look for trouble in the world. This, we know, won't be too difficult. All we have to do is turn on the news or read a local newspaper to see a thousand needs that aren't being met. Most likely, your church has a number of organizations they're partnering with to serve those in need. Ask a pastor or leader at your church to help you get connected. Or simply search the Internet for local organizations that can help you get off the sideline and make a difference. The key is to keep your eyes open and ask God to guide you, and you will find ways to get off the sideline and to get in the game.

Running to Trouble

Once you've spotted trouble, you get to the part that really takes courage: running to trouble.

I mentioned in the introduction to this book that the first sermon I preached in light of Hurricane Harvey came from two short verses:

> Blessed be the God and Father of our Lord Jesus Christ, the Father of mercies and the God of all comfort. He comforts us in all our affliction, so that we may

be able to comfort those who are in any kind of affliction, through the comfort we ourselves receive from God. (2 Cor. 1:3–4)

You may not feel you have what it takes to run to trouble. You may not feel like you have it in you to be a difference maker. Let me take some pressure off you: *you don't!* Well, let me clarify: You don't by yourself.

But you are not by yourself. Remember we are God's people, the sheep of his pasture, and are never alone because we have the Holy Spirit and we have one another. Together with the church and with the power of the Holy Spirit, we can run to trouble. We do not have to be afraid. We don't have to retreat to safety, comfort, or ease. We can get off the sidelines and get in the game. We can stop watching and start acting. And we can do so because the comfort that we bring to others who are afflicted is the comfort that we receive from God.

God is described here by the apostle Paul as "the Father of mercies and the God of all comfort." And he's *your* Father. He's *your* God. He has shown you infinite mercy and grants you a miraculous amount of comfort in the gospel, but remember, we were never meant to be cul-de-sacs of God's comfort; we're supposed to be conduits. The comfort of the gospel was never meant to get stuck in the church—it's meant to go *to* the church and then *to* the world *through* the church. You have received the comfort of God in Christ so that you can act. God has comforted you so that you can go looking for trouble—in the Word and in the world—and run to it with a loving heart and open hands, ready to serve in any and every way you can.

So, start with "yes" this week.

Teach the class, serve, give, hand a bottle of water to a homeless man at the stoplight, share your faith with a co-worker, pray for and with a friend, visit a neighbor, text a verse or prayer . . . put this chapter into practice and run to some trouble in the power and name of Jesus!

CHAPTER 9

Asleep in the Storm

Hurricane Harvey was the most devastating storm I have ever witnessed. I've talked about it much in this book already. It was a defining moment in our city and in my life and leadership. The financial toll on our city, the number of lives lost, the final tally of offices, church buildings, and homes destroyed—it was all too much to take in.

While rains of this severity only touch the US mainland once every several years, hurricanes continue throughout the world every year. The northwest Pacific Ocean, where these storms are called typhoons, experiences the most each year. In this part of the world, countries like Vietnam, Malaysia, Indonesia, the Philippines, China, and Japan are affected by storms year-round. One storm, the Great Bhola Cyclone, killed about a half a million people in Bangladesh.[1]

Hurricanes aren't the only kind of natural disaster that can do unspeakable damage. As I write, northern California wildfires continue to rage, decimating neighborhoods and open country alike. More than forty-five hundred firefighters have been engaged for two weeks, yet the fires remain. So far, seven people have been killed.[2]

If these tragic disasters accomplish anything, they certainly remind us of how powerless we are. When faced with a hurricane, a wildfire, a tornado, or a hailstorm, what can we do? We've developed technology that will now help us predict when these storms are coming, but we can do nothing to stop them. If we're lucky, we can insure our houses and evacuate towns when necessary, but no human being can command the mighty power of a rushing wind, the immense strength of the ocean's waves, or the indiscriminate pelting of a summer hailstorm.

Yet there is one who can. Jesus Christ, the unique God-man, the ultimate difference maker, showed that he had power even over the wind and the waves. On one stormy day at sea with his disciples, as they were overwhelmed by the immensity of what threatened to capsize their boat, Jesus spoke a calm over the wind and the water. But before he did, he took a nice, peaceful nap.

Asleep on the Boat

You can find this account in Matthew 8:23–27. Jesus has been going about doing public ministry. He's just healed several people in Capernaum, and then tells his disciples to get into the boat to go to the other side of the sea. This is where we pick up:

> As he got into the boat, his disciples followed him. Suddenly, *a violent storm arose on the sea*, so that the boat was being swamped by the waves—but Jesus kept sleeping. (Matt. 8:23–24, emphasis added)

Now, when you know how this story ends, it's pretty hilarious what Jesus is doing here. When you know he's going to wake up and rebuke the sea, it's like the nap is just setting him up for his mic-drop moment. But the disciples didn't know what was coming. They were terrified, and of all the appropriate ways to respond to a massive storm, sleeping was definitely not one of them.

Here's Jesus, our fearless leader, the guy we've given up our lives to follow, and now we're just going to go down without a fight? He's still asleep as the waves crash.

This is how it often feels when we are in a storm. "God, where are you?" We desperately cry for rescue yet we feel alone. The murky clouds of doubt, anxiety, and depression roll in with the wind and waves. I want to encourage you—the Lord has a plan for his greater glory and your good. His love remains and so does his power. You are *going* to make it. His perceived sleep is not distance or disdain for you but patience for the proper time to calm the storm. So hang on; you will get your life back at some point.

I went through a particularly difficult storm that was worse and longer than I expected. Emotionally, I was drained; mentally, I was weary from thinking about it; but spiritually I was deepening. Don't hear that I was smiling, singing upbeat praise songs. I was actually kneeling in prayer crying out at two in the morning. But I just kept moving slowly forward, trusting Jesus to "awake" at the right time. Finally, one day I said out loud to the Lord, "I got my life back." Everything was not solved, but I was no longer consumed by the waves, and the sun was shining again. Instead of rocking in the boat, I felt like I was watching from the shore. There were still some dark clouds, but the sun was breaking though and I was standing on solid ground.

With this hope the disciples take action, knowing Jesus is the only rescue, so they race to him:

> So the disciples came and woke him up, saying, "Lord, save us! We're going to die!" (Matt. 8:25)

Reasonable response from the disciples here, if you ask me. For all they could tell, they absolutely were about to die. But Jesus' response doesn't show the same level of empathy you or I might have. In fact, he didn't seem to have much patience at all for their terrified state.

> He said to them, "Why are you afraid, you of little faith?" Then he got up and rebuked the winds and the sea, and there was a great calm. The men were amazed and asked, "What kind of man is this? Even the winds and the sea obey him!" (Matt. 8:26–27)

This is an amazing moment in the ministry of Jesus. He leads his disciples into a boat to go to the other side of the sea. While in the boat, a great storm arises and threatens to capsize the boat. The disciples are frightened; Jesus is sleeping. They wake him, he calms the storm, and what happens to the disciples? They become even *more* frightened. Mark 4 tells the same story, and instead of "the men were amazed," Mark tells us, "they were terrified" (v. 41).

How can we explain this increase in fear? Why were the disciples more frightened now that the storm had ceased? The answer lies in the question the disciples ask one another: "Who then is this? Even the wind and the sea obey him!" (Mark 4:41). When the wind and the waves obeyed Jesus, his disciples finally started to grasp who he was.

Psalm 89:8–9 says, "LORD God of Armies, who is strong like you, LORD? Your faithfulness surrounds you. You *rule* the raging *sea*; when its *waves* surge, you *still* them" (emphasis mine). Jesus' calming of the wind and the waves was an announcement that he was not merely a man, not merely a good moral teacher; no, Jesus was making announcement that he was God. Only God rules the raging sea, only God stills its waves, and Jesus had done just that. So why were the disciples terrified? Because they realized they were standing in the very presence of God. They were no longer afraid of the sea; now, they were in awe of the God of the universe who stood in their midst. Jesus is molding these common men into difference makers.

From this story, we can learn three things about the life of a difference maker. If we are going to be difference makers, we have to know that Jesus will lead us into the storm, through the storm, and out of the storm.

He Leads Us into the Storm

How did the disciples find themselves at sea in a storm? Jesus led them there. Matthew 8:23 says, "As he got into the boat, his disciples followed him." Jesus is God, which means he is all knowing. He knew that storm was going to arise, and he knew he was going to use it to reveal who he was to his disciples. He led them into the boat, and he led them into the storm.

Yow! Say it isn't so. Jesus led them into the storm?! I thought obedience brings blessing. It does in the long term, but it doesn't always feel like that in the short term. Following Christ can actually make life harder. Staying in the marriage is more difficult than leaving; being honest may cost you; being selfless may mean you come in second.

The painful lesson we learn is you can be walking in obedience and still get swamped. As my squall was beginning, I kept saying to my wife, Kelly, "I feel like God is leading me into a band saw." As the words left my mouth, I dipped my head and lifted my shoulders with a wincing expression to prepare. As excruciating as it is, God does lead us into storms and we must keep following.

The definition of *disciple* is a follower or learner. The disciples were simply doing their job. They were walking in obedience, following Jesus, seeking to learn from him, and as a result, they saw their lives flash before their eyes. You can be following Christ faithfully and still end up in a dreadful storm. Not a storm of sin of your own doing— that's a different ballgame in which confession and repentance are the themes. This is a storm of the submissive life of the believer.

One of the greatest lies that has crept into our thinking through nominal, cultural Christianity is that Jesus is just an additive to your life. Christianity is just something you add to the mix to make life a little better, a little easier, a little more moral, a little more successful. But that is a lie from Satan. If we think this way, we'll have no concept for suffering or facing difficulty. If we think that Christianity is just something to make our earthly lives a little more comfortable, when we face a storm, we'll do one of three things: (1) We'll begin to think that God is passive, because he's powerful enough to stop our storms, but has chosen not to. Consequently, we begin to resent him and grow cold toward him. (2) We'll begin to think that, although God is good and would like to get us out of the storm he's just not powerful enough to do so. When we think God's weak, though we may still like him, we won't love him, because we depend on our own strength. (3) We'll begin to doubt that God was ever real in the first place. We'll totally abandon him and think he can't hear us, can't answer our prayers, can't get us out of the storm, because he's not real.

But God is real. He is powerful. And he is good. And he brings us into storms, not because he's evil and not because he's powerless, but because he's using the storm to reveal himself to us more clearly.

Following Jesus doesn't necessarily mean that you're going to be really cheery and always have a little smile on your face. You can follow Jesus into times of deep darkness, times of suffering, times of depression, times of anxiety. And sometimes when you're there, it feels like he's asleep on the boat!

C. S. Lewis, the great twentieth-century author, wrote a book called *A Grief Observed* after the death of his wife, Joy. Listen to these bone-chilling words he wrote about the feeling that Jesus is asleep in the boat:

> When you are happy, so happy you have no sense of needing Him, so happy that you are tempted to feel His claims upon you as an interruption, if you remember yourself and turn to Him with gratitude and praise, you will be—or so it feels— welcomed with open arms. But go to Him when your need is desperate, when all other help is vain, and what do you find? A door slammed in your face, and a sound of bolting and double bolting on the inside. After that, silence.[3]

Have you ever felt like that? Like God was totally absent? Like your prayers in a time of suffering were hitting the roof and bouncing right back down to you?

We've all been there and we will all be there again, but we must remember that even though it seems Jesus is asleep in the boat, ignoring our cries for help, he is still there. He is still in control. He is still Lord.

He Leads Us through the Storm

Just as surely as Jesus leads us into the storm, he will lead us through the storm. This is perhaps the most terrifying part of the process. It's terrifying to be in the storm, but isn't it just as scary as the moment when you realize there's no going back? That's how life is for difference makers. When we face the storm, there's no turning back. The only way out is through. And Jesus leads us through the storm.

One of the most well-known passages in the Bible is Psalm 23. Verse 3 says, "He leads me in paths of righteousness . . ." (ESV). Then the next verse says, "Even though I walk *through* the valley of the shadow of death, I will fear no evil, for you are with me; your rod and your staff, they comfort me" (v. 4 ESV, emphasis added). Notice the connection: first, we are led in righteous paths; then we are in the valley. Righteousness leads to the valley. It's the Old Testament way of Jesus saying, "Hop in the boat and let's head to the storm." The psalmist doesn't say, "Lord, help me walk *around the valley* of the shadow of death." He doesn't say, "Lord, let me turn back so I can get *out of the valley* of the shadow of death." No, he knows the only way out is *through the valley*. And what gives him the courage to keep walking? The presence of the Lord. "I will fear no evil, for you are with me; your rod and your staff, they comfort me." As Winston Churchill said, "If you are going through hell . . . keep going."[4]

The psalmist could keep walking because he knew God was there. God's rod and staff were there to protect him, to keep him close, to fend off enemies. The same was true for the disciples. Whether they knew it at the time of the storm or not, the disciples were on a boat with the Captain of the universe! He was in their boat, and he is in yours too! We are in the presence of God. What, then, should we fear?

Friend, I don't know what storm Jesus is leading you through right now. Maybe it's the storm of a difficult marriage, infertility, or undesired singleness. Maybe it's the storm of that one temptation that won't go away, strife in your church, or joblessness. Maybe there's just not enough money in the bank or a loved one has recently passed away. Please hear me clearly: I don't say this to be trite or to ignore the serious storms of our lives, but there is only one comfort in the waves . . . the Lord of the universe is in the storm with us. His presence is near, and that is our comfort. He will get you to the other side of the sea. He will lead you through the storm.

He Leads Us Out of the Storm

Jesus leads us into the storm, he leads us through the storm, and finally, he leads us out of the storm. If you don't see all three of these, you won't see God correctly.

Some people are optimists by nature. They want to think there will never be any storms, and if one arises, they have the tendency to ignore it or pretend it's not there. They believe this third truth about the storm, but they have trouble believing the first two.

Other people by nature are pessimists. They have resigned themselves to a life of storms. They know Jesus leads us into storms, and they even know he's with us in storms, but they just don't think they will ever be led out of the storm. The only response is to stiffen up that upper lip, to "keep calm and carry on."

Whether you are Tigger or Eeyore, the truth of the gospel gives us a third way. The truth that Jesus leads us into, through, and out of the storm leads us not to naïve optimism or stoic pessimism, but to hopeful resolve. The Word of God promises that one day Jesus will lead us all out of the storm. There will be little storms in life— maybe the ones you're in right now. They don't feel little at the moment, but in a year or two (or less) you'll be out of them and you'll almost forget they ever happened. Jesus is faithful to lead us out of those storms. The pain will be a memory and your strengthened faith will still be a reality. God will turn your misery into your ministry to others. Our pain regularly precedes our power as difference makers.

But there are other storms where the lightning and thunder continue to crackle on the horizon. Grief, sickness, caring for someone in need—on the list can go. These storms can heal, subside, or become a new normal, but they also remain challenges. Paul asked for the thorn in his side to be removed three times. But ultimately, he had to learn to live with it and trust God's grace.

Thankfully we'll be through with all of these storms in heaven. The gospel tells us we can have hope, even in these dreadful winds and waves, because we know that they will one day be silenced.

> For we know that the one who raised the Lord Jesus will also raise us with Jesus . . . Therefore we do not give up. Even though our outer person is being destroyed, our inner person is being renewed day by day. For our momentary light affliction is producing for us an absolutely incomparable eternal weight of glory. So we do not focus

on what is seen, but on what is unseen.
For what is seen is temporary, but what is
unseen is eternal. (2 Cor. 4:14, 16–18)

Jesus Is the Place of Rest

Difference makers know and trust that Jesus leads us into, through, and out of the storm, and because of this, difference makers can be at peace during the most turbulent seasons of life.

One of the starkest witnesses of Christianity ought to be our peace during turbulent times. When things are crazy politically or culturally (which is always), Christians, of all people, ought to be the ones who keep their heads on straight. Why? Not because we're optimists and ignore the realities, nor because we're pessimists and resign ourselves to the realities; rather, we keep our heads on because we find rest not in the calm seasons of life, but in the person of Jesus Christ. We aren't dependent on our plan or personality but his power to bring our boat to shore.

Hebrews 4 talks of the Sabbath rest that believers have in Jesus. Those who have faith in him have entered into the promised rest of God. This means we can be content in him, confident in his finished work on the cross, and certain of the work that is yet to come when he returns to set things right once and for all. What hope do we have in this world? We can't put our hope in politicians and governments, in money or possessions, in health or fitness. All of these things are false sources of security. They will eventually go away, and what will we be left with?

Our only source of hope, our refuge and strong tower (Ps. 61:3), is Jesus Christ who is with us in the boat. When we are with him, we are with the God who created, sustains, and rules all things. He will finish the good work he started. He will bring us all the way home. When you are going through hell . . . keep going!

CHAPTER 10

Difference Makers Worship God All the Time

Can you make a difference when your life doesn't go the way you hope it will? This is the question that all of us will face at one point or another. It's the question that the Charleston, South Carolina's Emanuel AME Church faced in the summer of 2015.

During Wednesday night Bible study, members of this church were gathered to worship, to encourage one another, and to learn from God's Word. In the midst of their gathering, the unthinkable happened, as a young man named Dylann Roof, who had sat through almost an hour of the Bible study, stood up and opened fire, killing nine. Only five survived. "In an instant," as one reporter put it, "wives lost husbands, fathers lost daughters, children lost parents, and a church lost its pastor."[1]

Clearly, this was not the way the members of that church saw their Wednesday night Bible study going; more significantly, it was not the way the members of that church saw their lives going. A gaping void was left—for some, family members, for all, beloved friends, brothers and sisters in Christ.

The members of Emanuel AME Church asked: *Can we make a difference even when life doesn't go the way we hoped it would?* Their answer was a resounding yes.

> Two days later, as the nation simmered with outrage and disbelief, the families of those murdered by Roof were allowed, in accordance with the law for bond hearings, to speak by closed-circuit television to Roof. Television networks carried the feed from both rooms: the room where Roof stood, nearly expressionless, flanked by police; and the room where his victims' relatives were gathered. One after another, they spoke words of forgiveness even as their voices shook with grief and anger.[2]

Did this make a difference? Yes. These faithful, precious saints, from whom so much had been taken, made a profound difference. In a world of envy and anger, of grudge-holding, continued racial tensions, and revenge-seeking, these Christians did the unthinkable. They forgave.

This level of forgiveness does not make sense to the world, because in the world's economy, we can only make a difference when our lives go the way we hope and expect they will. We enjoy difference making when it is fun, inspiring and planned on the calendar, but this is a completely different level. Roxane Gray expressed her difficulty with forgiveness in a *New York Times* op-ed titled "Why I Can't Forgive Dylann Roof." While noting her deep respect for "the families of the nine slain who are able to forgive this terrorist," Gray explained:

> Forgiveness does not come easily to me. I am fine with this failing. I am particularly unwilling to forgive those who show no remorse, who don't demonstrate any interest in reconciliation.[3]

Gray is admittedly unwilling to move forward when no remorse is shown by the offending party—when there is no explanation, apology, or attempt to make right the wrongs that have been committed.

I don't cite Gray's remarks to condemn her; she is simply expressing what comes naturally to all of us. When we have been wronged intentionally or unintentionally by another person, when we have seemingly gotten the short end of the stick by chance, or when we have apparently been dealt a bad hand by God himself (when Jesus is taking us into the storm), we don't want to move forward until we've had an explanation, an apology, or an attempt to make things right.

Let's return to the Difference Maker Declaration:

> I was made for more than watching. I have a history-changing, difference-making, life-giving, *Spirit-empowered legacy to leave.* Jesus, I ask you to work deeply in me and clearly through me as I pray, give, and go in your love. I am a difference maker.

The only way we leave a "Spirit-empowered legacy" is when life is more than we can handle in our own strength. The families of the Charleston Nine so courageously displayed a potency that showed the power of the Holy Spirit in them. We can do the same by continuing to worship the Lord through thick and thin.

The Patience of Job

"There was a man in the country of Uz named Job. He was a man of complete integrity, who feared God and turned away from evil" (Job 1:1). Thus begins the Old Testament book named after its main character, Job.

The story of Job is so well known, even outside of Judaism and Christianity, that we refer in conversation to "the patience of Job." Job is a hallmark of patience because he bore suffering worse than most of us can even fathom, and he did so with integrity, refusing to let go of his faith in God.

Job was incredibly blessed by God. He had "seven sons and three daughters" (v. 2), "seven thousand sheep and goats, three thousand camels, five hundred yoke of oxen, five hundred female donkeys, and a very large number of servants" (v. 3). In other words, this guy was loaded.

Can such a man make a difference? Absolutely! Like Esther, use the power of your palace. "Job was the greatest man among all the people of the east" (v. 3).

But this story is not about a healthy, wealthy, prosperous man who made a difference with his health, wealth, and prosperity; it's about a healthy, wealthy, prosperous man who made a difference by losing his health, wealth, and prosperity, and worshiping God anyway. As his palace crumbled, his faith remained.

There is background to this story that Job isn't aware of—a conversation between Satan and God. Satan essentially accuses God of bribing Job for worship. "Job only worships you because you've given him all this stuff," Satan says (vv. 9–10, paraphrase). "But stretch out your hand and strike everything he owns, and he will surely curse you to your face" (v. 11). The whole story of Job, then, answers one question: Will Job remain faithful?

So God allows Satan to test Job. He allows him to make certain that Job's life doesn't go the way Job hoped it would go. As a result, Job lost his oxen, donkeys, and his servants (vv. 14–15), his sheep (v. 16), his camels (v. 17), his sons and daughters (vv. 18–19), his health (2:7), and his intimacy with his wife (2:10). Job lost everything but his own life.

Job Worships

How would you respond if you were in Job's shoes? We've got to be honest—if it were us instead of Job, I think Satan might have won the bet. Most people would have a very hard time not turning from God.

Remember what we said in the last chapter? If you view Christianity as just an additive in your life to make things a little better, when suffering comes, you'll either lose your trust in him because you think he's passive, lose your worship of him because you think he's powerless, or lose your faith in him because you think he's a fairy tale. But what about Job? Even in the midst of the most horrific suffering imaginable, Job *worshiped*! He knew that God was still God, that God was still good, powerful, and present.

Job 1:20–21 records Job's initial response to his suffering, and it is one of the most amazing passages in the entire Bible:

> Then Job stood up, tore his robe, and shaved his head. He fell to the ground and worshiped, saying: Naked I came from my mother's womb, and naked I will leave this life. The LORD gives, and the LORD takes away. Blessed be the name of the LORD.

In chapter 2, in the midst of her own suffering, Job's wife speaks differently. Now, the text doesn't tell us her intention. It's likely that she spoke out of her suffering and said something she didn't mean, something she would later regret. Nonetheless, she spoke wrongly, asking Job, "Are you still holding on to your integrity? Curse God and die!" (Job 2:9). But look at Job's response: "Should we accept only good from God and not adversity?" (v. 10). More worship. More submission to God's sovereign plan. Job worshiped God all the time.

Job knew that God was still God, even in his suffering, and that led him to worship. Even though he had lost everything, even though his possessions were taken from him, his family was taken from him, and his health was taken from him, Job *worshiped*. The pain was real. His kids had names and personalities. They were loved by their father, rocked to sleep by their mother, and gathered around the dinner table for family meals. So with a torn robe, shaved head, and falling to the ground, Job kept his faith. Don't pass this by as just some story from the past. See it with the eyes of a neighbor watching cars and casseroles arrive at the house across the street after the funeral as you ache wondering how you can help.

I've Seen It Firsthand

We all know a Job. As a pastor I may know more than most. Pastoring is an unusual job for many reasons, but one is dealing with death and funerals on a consistent basis. How often is a black hearse parked outside the door of where you work? Not an unusual sight when you are employed at a church. Some funerals are a celebration of a long life of impact and others are the deep grief of a life cut short.

When I walked into the Barfields' house that afternoon, the grief was thick. Worship music was playing and hugs were easy to find. Warren, at thirteen years old, died in an ATV accident while having fun with his family over Thanksgiving. He was an amazing young man who loved the Lord. He would actually write sermons from passages of Scripture he liked. Not a lot of teenage boys do that. He had a great smile and could hit a baseball like a pro.

I remember my son playing against him as Warren went 2 for 3 with a couple of runs batted in. Great kid, great family . . . great grief.

I've walked with his parents, Bill and Julie, through this Job-like event, and they have responded in worship. What an encouragement to watch them continue to parent their daughter, Grace, and grow closer than ever in their marriage. The Barfields sit on the third row, front and center, each Sunday. I usually join the worship team on the stage for the last song before I speak. My mic is thankfully off, but I'm still singing to the Lord and looking out at our people, getting a feel for the room before I preach; often Bill and Julie catch my eye. Their eyes are closed but their hearts are wide open. Many times I've seen tears rolling down Julie's cheeks as Bill puts his arm around her.

Through the pain, they continue to worship—not just sing; anyone can sing. They *worship* Christ. God is using their worship to fuel being difference makers. For example, they helped a student worship event called "IGNiTE" at the public high school Grace attends and Warren would have attended. They have shared their testimony of God's faithfulness numerous times with others on a hard path. God is making a huge difference through them as their misery becomes ministry.

A few weeks ago I noticed a woman crying across the aisle from me. Her son had died recently. I gave her a hug and told her I wanted her to meet someone. At the end of the service I introduced her to Julie. Truly, the Barfields understood this couple's pain.

Worship is a weapon for good in our grief and difficulties. We have to continue to worship and trust Christ to bring good from our pain. He has done that for the Barfields. During Warren's memorial service, many of his peers trusted Christ as Savior. Julie's blog[4] is read by countless people; they have been difference makers in their kid's school and a blessing to our church body. This doesn't negate the pain or suggest Warren isn't missed tremendously. There is still an empty seat at the table, but it does illustrate the power of worshiping God and accepting his will even in the pain. This is what difference-maker legacies are made of.

Listen to Julie's words to me recently:

> Our day-to-day can be pretty messy and sometimes complicated as we each walk our own path of grief and healing. I cannot imagine ever missing Warren less, but what I have observed is that in my own personal journey my focus has shifted. My focus is less about Warren and more about Jesus. For example, I don't crumble

in the grocery store when I pass his favorite Double Stuffed Oreo Cookies . . . but rather I am able to see more clearly how God is working, using Warren, and our testimony that God is good, for kingdom purpose.[5]

Will You Commit to Worship God All the Time?

Many Bible scholars believe Job was written earlier than any other book of the Bible, and that the story it contains took place before the year 2000 BC. That means Job lived more than four thousand years ago, and we're still talking about him. Clearly, then, this man made a difference. His integrity and patience in suffering is still talked about these four thousand years later.

In Job 17, the sufferer uttered the words, "My days have slipped by; my plans have been ruined, even the things dear to my heart" (v. 11). Job's life did not go the way he thought it would go. Yet he was a difference maker because even though life wasn't what he thought it would be, he continued to worship God. That's what difference makers do.

Will you commit to worshiping God all the time? Will you decide now that whatever comes your way, good or bad, you will always worship him?

Friend, the difference you make in the world has nothing to do with how many people know who you are, are aware of your work, or follow you on social media. All of those things will fade away. They are all temporal, and a hundred years after you die, they're unlikely to be remembered. The difference you make isn't ultimately measured in these categories, but in your faithful worship of God, who will make the difference through you.

The difference you make might not be something you see in your lifetime. In the second to last song of Lin-Manuel Miranda's *Hamilton: The Musical*, Alexander Hamilton ponders his legacy in the seconds before his death. "What is a legacy?" He asks. "It's planting seeds in a garden you never get to see."[6] Are you content to worship God even if your legacy is something you never get to see? Even if the difference you make is only felt after you are gone?

In chapter 7, we said that true worship, as defined by Paul in Romans 12, is giving *everything*—our whole selves—to God for him to use as he pleases. That, ultimately, is the legacy of a difference maker. And this is the challenge I issue to you.

Whether you're a mom or a dad, a son or a daughter, I challenge you to be a difference maker by worshiping God all the time.

Whether you're rich or poor, strong or weak, I challenge you to be a difference maker by worshiping God all the time.

Whether you're a student, a pastor, or a lawyer, an accountant, a technician, or a janitor, I challenge you to be a difference maker by worshiping God all the time.

We can't control the things that happen to us in life. We don't decide our life circumstances. We don't dictate which storms Jesus will take us into or how long it will take to get through them. But we are in control of our response, and our response determines whether we will be difference makers.

Difference Makers

The world needs difference makers more than anything else. We saw in chapter 3 that difference making starts with the heart, that difference makers have courage, and that difference makers point to their Savior. In chapter 4 we learned that difference makers dine in diversity and speak with clarity. Chapter 5 taught us that in Christ, difference makers have a new and secure identity, are never alone, and are unashamed of who they are and whose they are. Esther taught us that difference makers ought to strive for the palace, and once we're there, risk it all for the glory of God and the good of others. Ezra taught us that difference makers give and go for Jesus. In chapter 8, we learned that difference makers run to trouble. Chapter 9 taught us that difference makers have peace in the storm because of the presence of Jesus. And now, we see that difference makers, like Job, worship God all the time.

So are you ready? Are you ready to dive in? To get off the sidelines of life? I truly believe that God has a plan to make a difference in you and through you if you'll let him. He's not content with us being fans of Jesus; he wants us to be followers. He's not content with nominal Christianity that cheers on the difference makers from the sidelines; he wants us to be all in. Are you ready to make that commitment? Are you ready to be a difference maker? Let's do it! Step up and out for the ride of your life. It's not easy, but definitely worth it!

You were made for more than watching. You really are a history changer and difference maker. Your life will give life to others as you walk in the power of the Holy Spirit. God wants to leave a legacy through your short time on earth that shapes your great-great grandkids, your workplace, and your church. Keep asking Jesus to work in you, even more in the hard times, and you'll see him work through you in amazing ways. He'll use your prayers, sacrifice, and steps of faith to give you the courage to say . . . I am a difference maker!

Bill, Julie, Warren, and Grace Barfield during their last Christmas together in Tennessee.

CHAPTER 11

Difference Makers Don't Sleep Well

It's 3:47 a.m. on Tuesday morning. My Apple Watch says my heart rate is 89 BPM. Why in the world am I up and stressed? A week ago, yesterday and today were scheduled on the calendar to be off days.

Somehow the schedule has again swamped my rest. Is there really ever a day off for a difference maker? I don't want you to finish this book and think making a difference is going to be easy or come without a price. Our desire for impact and change starts with a burden and results in a lot of work and . . . worry.

How do you tell your mind to no longer have thoughts? How do you tell your heart to no longer have passion? How do you walk the life of faith without waking up in the wee hours realizing the risk? Difference makers don't sleep well; they think and care deeply, and that's not defined by the clock. It's like Paul said to his Corinthian audience: "Apart from other things, there is the daily pressure on me of my anxiety for all the churches" (2 Cor. 11:28 ESV). This anxiety came from knowing his weakness. "Who is weak, and I am not weak?" (v. 29 ESV).

Difference makers know that God has equipped them for an incredible journey that will bring about positive change in the world, but they know they're completely dependent on God to move the mountains. By ourselves, difference makers are, well, not difference makers. We're weak. And that's at least part of why we don't sleep well.

I'm not sure how many times through the years the house has been quiet and my mind has been active. Finally at some point I give in to the restless ache and roll out of bed, headed with a Bible and journal to the nearest sofa. Prayer on my knees and then a Bible in my lap. A journal and pen asking the Lord what's going on and what he wants to tell me.

I don't think you can be a difference maker without burning the midnight oil at times. We hear of the great saints praying through the night, but somehow we think we will escape. Hudson Taylor, the powerful missionary to China, committed to praying from 2:00 to 4:00 a.m. each morning. This was the time "when he could be most sure of being undisturbed to wait upon God."[1] Sleepless nights are unavoidable for someone who wants to make a difference. "Couldn't you stay awake with me for one hour? Stay awake and pray . . ." (Matt. 26:40–41).

I wish I could say all of these prayer times were a remembrance of my blessings, deep faith, or at least a celebration of the goodness of God. But more often than not, they are times the weeds of worry grow faster than you can uproot. They're times spent presenting my requests to God, hoping that "the peace of God, which surpasses all understanding, will guard [my heart and mind] in Christ Jesus" (Phil. 4:7). They're times spent reminding myself to "consider the birds of the sky. . . . Observe how the wildflowers of the field grow" (Matt. 6:26, 28). If God cares for these things, won't he care for me as well? Sometimes these prayer times are spent crying out with David, "How long, LORD? Will you forget me forever? How long will you hide your face from me? How long will I store up anxious concerns within me, agony in my mind every day?" (Ps. 13:1–2).

These late-night worries are often washed away by the sunrise. The issues are not as overwhelming in the daylight as they seemed in the dark. But it doesn't mean that this was wasted time. It is a place of spiritual growth—the place from which the power of a true leader comes.

Many who wake up and worry through the night may try to quell their anxiety by surfing the Internet or reading a book until they fall asleep. But the leader wakes up to soil his knees and call upon a great God to meet him at that moment. He declares one more time, "Not my will, but yours, be done." Tears are in the eyes and prayers are released from the lips in the midst of walking in the unknown, reminding ourselves all the while, "Even when I go through the darkest valley, I fear no danger, for you are with me; your rod and your staff—they comfort me" (Ps. 23:4).

What kinds of anxieties will get you out of bed as a difference maker? Pick your poison.

Often, family troubles will get you out of bed. A child or parent or sibling is still rejecting God, though they've heard the gospel a thousand times. Someone is in trouble at school; someone is slipping back into drugs or alcohol; someone's marriage is on the fence.

It could be a problem at work. There's a big project coming up and you know you need to perform well. There's a new employee you're training who is struggling to make the progress you were hoping they would make. This quarter's financials aren't looking like you thought, and you are on your way to missing budget.

Or it could just be the problems in our society, in our world. There's been another mass shooting. There's been another high-profile act of hate. There's been more political unrest in our nation or abroad. There's been another natural disaster. How can you stay in bed, comfortably asleep, without a care in the world, when *all this* is going on around you?

How things will turn out is not truly the issue. God is in control. He is sovereign. The issue is, *Will I wake up and call upon God in the middle of the night? Will he be more important than sleep? Will I trust him with tomorrow's energy as I've pleaded tonight in prayer?*

God knows what we need before we ask him. He is in control of the ends and the means, whether we get out of bed and pray or not. But he wants us to come to him, like a little child, begging him to provide, pleading that he will give us the wisdom, the direction, the help we need. Why? Because these are the moments when difference makers are forged. It's not the stage or the award ceremony in which we grow. Leaders are forged where no one sees and their heart is racing inside them. The place where fear gives way to faith and humility is victorious over pride.

Leaders are forged at 3:47 a.m. It's in the soil of the dark night of the soul that the seeds of morning flowers will blossom.

It's the ache of the mother's heart that calls her room by room praying for children at night. It's the tears of the father asking for more than just their kids making good grades and staying off drugs but that they deeply walk with God. It's the prayers of the night and the pleading to God that deepen the parent in ways we cannot see and in the spiritual realm that grow the children while they sleep.

The prayers of the night call the muster for the angels amassing for the victory of the next day. The prayers of the night are the sincerest, calling out far beyond eloquent words and "bless this food to the good of our bodies . . ." prayers. The unscripted ache is more precious in the sight of God than the crafted sentence. Even when we don't know how to pray, we groan, and the Spirit intercedes for us. These are the prayers that shape us.

If you want to sleep well, don't be a difference maker. If you want to sleep well, ignore what's going on around you. Put your head in the sand. Stay away from the headlines. Stay away from hard conversations. Stay away from anything meaningful. Stay detached and don't get your heart in the game. Not just because leaders worry, but because leaders care. They ache, they cry, and they hurt, but sometimes, many times, they celebrate more deeply than those who sleep peacefully. They know the battles that have been won because they were there, awake, on their knees, fighting for the victory.

This morning I've been in leadership for more than thirty years. I've seen God perform more than I can ever imagine, and yet, I ache, pray, and wonder what he will do next. I wait on him, believing that "those who trust in the LORD will renew their strength" (Isa. 40:31). I've seen it happen before, and I trust I'll see it again. And when I do, I'll celebrate, because I was there calling for help in the midst of the battle.

Jesus is better than sleep. Prayers are better than dreams. Kneeling is better than lying down. The difference maker must understand that sleepless nights have great purpose in forming their character, great influence in shaping their future, and great impact on eternity.

Thank you, Lord, for waking me up. Every hour is yours, and you can call me to prayer any time you want. Inconvenient hours are yours, my sleep is yours, and thankfully, my problems are yours as well. So I take the ache in my heart and give it to you in full trust and confidence that you're at work. You always are.

———

Ahh, I feel better already. At the end of writing this, according to my Apple Watch, my heart rate is back down to 67 BPM. It's 4:43 a.m. An hour of sleep missed, but seeds of prayer and deeper character development captured.

Difference makers don't always sleep well, but Jesus is better than sleep.

New, Not Just Improved

Each year when the holidays have passed and we turn the calendars over for a fresh start, millions of people make resolutions. There are whole industries built around this, and marketers have pinpointed how to sell to the "new year, new you" hysteria. But have you ever seen a new year really make a new you?

Think about it. What do most New Year's resolutions revolve around? Health. We resolve to be more healthy people. We're going to exercise more, so we buy new running shoes and join a new gym. We're going to eat better, so we buy a bunch of kale and purchase a new calorie-counting app. In the best cases, we lose ten or fifteen or twenty pounds, build some muscle, and feel more energized. In most cases, we give up on our resolutions by February and have a little less money in our bank accounts. (The marketers got the best of us!)

Other New Year's resolutions revolve around spirituality or morality. "I'm going to go to church more," we say. "I'm going to give more. I'm going to read my Bible more." Of course, all of these are good things, and I recommend them. But if the focus is on being "good," we're missing the point. Again, at best, we're a little nicer and feel a bit better about ourselves; more than likely, we've ditched the Bible-in-a-year plan by February and feel like we're just not good enough Christians.

The reality is, New Year's resolutions don't work very often because they aim too low. They're marketed as "new year, new you" plans, but they're really "new year, improved you" plans. But we don't simply need to be improved; we need to be made new.

That's the purpose of this book. I hope and pray you don't walk away from these pages convinced you're going to make a difference without the power of God through his Holy Spirit. As a Christian, believing in his saving work for you on the cross, you've been given a new heart. You've been made new, not just improved. With the Holy Spirit living in you and joining together with the people of God . . . there's nothing standing between you and making a difference!

There's no telling what it will look like. Maybe you'll see the fruit of it in this life; maybe you won't. Maybe it'll be a difference that a ton of people notice; maybe only a few people will notice. Maybe it will be easy; maybe it will be the hardest thing you've ever done. But two things are certain: you'll know God better because of it, and you won't regret it for a second.

This is the life you want—a challenging life, sure, but a life of significance. This is what our churches and nation need—not pew sitters, but difference makers. Your kids, neighbors, spouse, friends, and coworkers are longing for you to step up and step out. Join something, start something, volunteer, love, care, pray, go for it. It's time; it's the right time; it's your time to be a difference maker.

Starting today, say it and live it with all you've got . . .

I was made for more than watching. I have a history-changing, difference-making, life-giving, Spirit-empowered legacy to leave. Jesus, I ask you to work deeply in me and clearly through me as I pray, give, and go in your love. I am a difference maker!

Notes

Introduction

1. https://www.climate.gov/news-features/event-tracker/reviewing-hurricane-harveys-catastrophic-rain-and-flooding

Chapter 1

1. https://www.cdc.gov/nchs/data/hus/hus16.pdf#019
2. https://www.cnbc.com/2016/12/22/as-heart-disease-deaths-rise-health-experts-focus-on-prevention.html
3. Millard Erickson, *Christian Theology,* 3rd ed. (Grand Rapids, MI: Baker, 2013), 256.
4. John Owen, *The Mortification of Sin* (public domain).
5. Ibid.

Chapter 2

1. http://nytimesineducation.com/spotlight/what-the-world-needs-now/
2. https://www.britannica.com/art/score-music
3. https://twitter.com/EarlLavender/status/1019585296181194752

Chapter 3

1. https://www.freedomchurchalliance.org
2. Ibid.

3. https://www.bibleplaces.com/capernaum/

Chapter 4

1. https://www.businessinsider.com/best-food-instagram-2016-12
2. https://readingacts.com/2010/10/10/galatians-211-14-what-is-table-fellowship/
3. Mark L. Strauss, *Four Portraits, One Jesus: An Introduction to Jesus and the Gospels* (Grand Rapids, MI: Zondervan, 2007), 133.
4. https://www.wsj.com/articles/divided-america-stands-then-and-now-1498851654

Chapter 5

1. https://www.preachingtoday.com/illustrations/1997/april/3121.html
2. "Slide," by The Goo Goo Dolls, *Dizzy Up the Girl* (1998).
3. Timothy Keller, *Making Sense of God* (New York, NY: Penguin, 2016), 134.

Chapter 6

1. https://www.placeministries.org. This is the tool we use at HFBC.
2. https://www.barnesandnoble.com/p/a-guide-to-christian-ambition-hugh-hewitt/1111521301/2672298865333?st=PLA&sid=BNB_DRS_New+Marketplace+Shopping+Books_000 00000&2sid=Google_&sourceId=PLGoP212653&gclid=EAI aIQobChMIu_2Ko9u43QIVhcDACh3vwAGiEAQYASABEgI xavD_BwE, page 21.
3. These are two ministries that the author supports: http://uttermostinternational.org and http://familylegacy.com.

Chapter 7

1. Elisabeth Elliot, *Shadow of the Almighty: The Life and Testament of Jim Elliot* (Peabody, MA: Hendrickson Publishers, Inc., 2008), 15.

2. Art Rainer, *The Money Challenge* (Nashville, TN: B&H Publishing, 2017), 16.

3. https://www.sebts.edu/

4. http://www.espn.com/espn/page2/story/_/page/gallo%2 F110517_NCAA_commencement

5. C. S. Lewis, *The Weight of Glory* (1949; repr., New York: HarperCollins, 1980), 26.

6. https://www.desiringgod.org/articles/driving-convic tions-behind-foreign-missions

Chapter 8

1. https://www.cdc.gov/vhf/ebola/history/2014-2016-outbreak /index.html

2. https://www.christianexaminer.com/article/despite -growing-african-ebola-crisis-ministries-keep-going-serving- there/47447.htm

3. https://www.thegospelcoalition.org/article/how-south- ern-baptists-trained-more-disaster-relief-volunteers-than-the- red-cross/

4. https://www.usatoday.com/story/news/politics/2017/09 /10/hurricane-irma-faith-groups-provide-bulk-disaster -recovery-coordination-fema/651007001/

5. Francis Chan, *Crazy Love* (Colorado Springs, CO: David C. Cook, 2013), 76.

Chapter 9

1. https://ocean.si.edu/planet-ocean/waves-storms-tsunamis/ hurricanes-typhoons-and-cyclones

2. https://www.npr.org/2018/08/05/635789040/california-fires-spread-rapidly-killing-seventh-victim

3. C. S. Lewis, *A Grief Observed* (1961; repr., New York, NY: HarperCollins, 1994), 5–6.

4. https://www.forbes.com/sites/geoffloftus/2012/05/09/if-youre-going-through-hell-keep-going-winston-churchill/#1caeb882d549.

Chapter 10

1. https://www.christianitytoday.com/ct/2016/june/cover-story-standing-with-charleston-after-emanuel-church-s.html

2. Ibid.

3. https://www.nytimes.com/2015/06/24/opinion/why-i-cant-forgive-dylann-roof.html

4. http://www.risinguppsalm115.org/

5. Used by permission.

6. Lin-Manuel Miranda, "The World Was Wide Enough," *Hamilton: The Musical* (2015).

Chapter 11

1. Dr. and Mrs. Howard Taylor, *Hudson Taylor's Spiritual Secret* (Chicago, IL: Moody, 1989), 239.